DRAGONS
AND
SERPENTS

In this important book, Stefan Broennle affords readers a glimpse into the origins of our terrestrial world that resists being devoured by the dragon mythology of past cultures. Dragons and dragon-serpents instead feature as co-creators of a reality that we experience daily, wholly unaware that we are walking through the jaws of the dragon. The book helps us to recognize dragons as entities without which there would be no structure to time or space and no conditions in which life on Earth could evolve as a miracle of incarnation. Stefan Broennle closes with an invitation to be open to sensing these primordial forces of Earth's creation for ourselves and to allow them to enrich our own lives.

Marko Pogačnik,
UNESCO Artist for Peace (2016–2022)

DRAGONS
AND
SERPENTS

Earth Mysteries
and the
Time of Change

Stefan Broennle

EARTHDANCER

AN INNER TRADITIONS IMPRINT

First edition 2024
Dragons and Serpents
Earth Mysteries and the Time of Change
Stefan Broennle

This English edition © 2024 Earthdancer GmbH
English translation © 2024 JMS books LLP
Editing by JMS books LLP (www.jmseditorial.com)

Originally published in German as:
Drache und Schlange, in Symbolik, Geomantie und der aktuellen Wandelzeit
World © 2023 Neue Erde GmbH, Saarbruecken, Germany

Cover images: Inkling Design (dragon), pinholeimaging (landscape), Color Symphony (texture), FrentaN (snake bas relief), all shutterstock.com
Cover design, typesetting, and layout: Dragon Design UK
Typeset in Minion

Printed and bound in Germany by Appel & Klinger

Cataloging-in-Publication Data for this title is available from the Library of Congress.

ISBN 979-8-88850-073-6 (print)
ISBN 979-8-88850-083-5 (ebook)

Published by Earthdancer, an imprint of Inner Traditions
www.earthdancerbooks.com, www.innertraditions.com

MIX
Paper from
responsible sources
FSC
www.fsc.org   FSC® C100257

Contents

Introduction: The Path to the Dragon's Cave   7

The Symbolism of the Serpent   9
Nagas: The Serpent and the Consciousness of the Earth   9
The Woman and the Serpent   12
The Bird and the Serpent   16
The Tale of the White Snake   18

The Meaning of the Dragon   26
The Dragon as a Bringer of Culture   28
The Chinese Dragon   31
The Legacy of the Dragon   33
The Laughing Buddha and the Dragon   34
The Dragon's Hoard   36
The Dragon and the Stars   38
When Christians Heal Dragons   41
Gaia and the Dragon   43

Famous Dragons   46
Fáfnir   46
The Hydra   47
The Red Dragon of Wales   49
Nidhogg   50
Apopis   52
Nessie   53

The Dragon in Geomantic Symbolism   55
Dragon Paths   64
Ley Lines   66
Dragon Lines   69
Soul Paths   72
Soul Water   74

A Time of Change and a Time of Dragons:
When the Dragons Rise   78
The Shadow of the Dragon   78
Free Dragons   81
A Time of Change: A Time of Chaos   83
When Gaia Awakens   86
The Power of the Serpent as a Path to Healing   89
A Time of Change: Opening Dragon Portals   91
A Time of Change: Dreaming of Serpents   96
A Time of Change: Stormy Nights   99

Awaken the Dragon Within!   **102**

Picture Credits   106
About the Author   107

Introduction:
The Path to the Dragon's Cave

I am writing this book as 2021 draws to a close, having experienced all the pressures and difficulties of the past two years, a time during which, as far as I am concerned, society turned away from both reason and Nature. Consequently, some of the content could be considered outdated at a later point in time, although I do not anticipate this, or instead could be overtaken by events, which I think is more likely to be the case. On a symbolic level, I see human behavior during the years of the Covid pandemic and even today, and the political measures imposed against the virus, of which only the tiniest minority could be termed "medical," as reflecting much of our relationship with the Earth, and indeed with dragons, with the fight against the virus resembling the much-vaunted fight against the dragons.

We are familiar with these legendary dragons. They are battled as foes in novels such as JRR Tolkien's *The Hobbit* (with its dragon, Smaug), or in films such as the post-apocalyptic *Reign of Fire*, or *Eragon* and *DragonHeart* where they become close friends with humans. There is no doubt that the way we view dragons is changing, but is there any point in even thinking about them in an age of computer chips and digital worlds? Aren't dragons and giant primordial serpents little more than leftovers from fairy tales and children's books, just myths from a time when it was impossible to imagine certain natural phenomena in any other way?

I believe that this is selling ourselves short. Dragons and serpents are deeply entwined with humanity's myths and are part of human existence itself. They do indeed represent a higher reality. . . .

But we are getting ahead of ourselves. To begin, I would like to introduce the dragon as a metaphor, an archetypal symbol, in order to explore the close connection between humans and dragons, and humans and serpents. We will first limit ourselves to an examination of the dragon as an important symbol.

If you are happy to join me on the journey, I would like to take you deeper into the dragon's cave and allow the dragon symbol to be revealed as a palpable force in geomancy, and to use this insight to depict dragons and serpents as creative forces currently undergoing a fundamental transformation that is guiding human beings and the Earth into a new relationship with each other. In this way, dragon power becomes a field of collective consciousness that is more essential now than ever before as both the Earth and humanity find themselves in an era of change.

Follow me into the depths of the dragon's cave where I hope we will discover the dragon's hoard, a precious treasure deep in the bowels of the Earth.

What connects these two animal symbols? The dragon and the serpent or snake (both of which are described with the Greek word *drákōn*) were sacred to the Earth Mother, the Great Goddess, and large serpents were often kept in the temples of the goddess. Recent finds in Anatolia suggest a tradition of serpent worship that stretches back 11,000 years. Stone pillars with relief carvings depicting snakes in the Neolithic archeological site Göbekli Tepe in Turkey have been dated to 9000 BCE. The Mesopotamian goddess Ereshkigal, her son Ninazu, his son Ningishzida, Tishpak, Ninazu's successor, the patron city god of Susa, and (last but not least) Ištaran, are all associated with serpent symbolism, and during the course of this book we will encounter many such gods who are closely related with images of serpents and dragons. The dragon represented the annual seasonal plant life cycle and became a symbol of rebirth, as did the serpent, which sheds and renews its skin. The legends of both the dragon and the serpent therefore often came to represent the elemental power of the Earth and the cycle of the seasons.

The Symbolism of the Serpent

We are of course aware of the wicked serpent from the Garden of Eden as the incarnation of evil in Christian iconography, so instead we will head to Asia, where even to this day the relationship between human beings and snakes is depicted in a positive light.

Nagas: The Serpent and the Consciousness of the Earth

The Earth (all matter) bears a consciousness within itself, a consciousness that has the potential for a divinity of its own. In Asia it is symbolized by the nagas. *Naga* means "serpentine" and the feminine form is *nagini* (as we know, Nagini is the name of Lord Voldemort's serpent ally in the *Harry Potter* novels). In Indian folk religion, the nagas are highly revered chthonic (underworld) divinities and the guardians of the home. In southern India women draw the intricate pattern known as the *kalam* in front of the entrances to their homes in a ritual intended to invite in the nagas and invoke their powers of fertility.

Naga worship spread throughout Asia, where they are depicted as serpents, humans with a serpent's head or tail, or as serpents with many heads.

Fig. 1. Nagas as guardians of the threshold.

Nagas as the power of the Earth or of a place

Nagas are said to live in various specific places around the world. For example, the Yanzhog Yumco, the largest lake in Tibet, is said to be the home of the naga kings, while Shesha, one of the most famous of the nagas, supports and carries the Earth itself (suggesting a connection with the Norse Midgard Serpent, *Miðgarðsormr*). In Thailand, however, nagas live in the mountains or in ornate palaces at the bottom of rivers, lakes, and seas, where they are protectors of the consciousness of the Earth and its spiritual treasures. The legendary Mount Meru, the mountain of worlds, connects the various levels of being as the *axis mundi*, the world axis. Nagas also live within it as protectors, just as the dragon Nidhogg (*Niðhöggr)* from Norse mythology lives in the roots of the sacred tree Yggdrasil. In India, before the foundation stone for a new house is laid, a geomantic practitioner searches for the point where the naga's head is located and marks it with a post. By using this marker to lay the foundation stone, the house is connected with the power of the Earth.

Nagas can also signify a mountain, plant, or tree, as nagas dwell within all these.

Nagas as symbols of consciousness

In the Hindu tradition, Vishnu, in the form of Narayana, lies in cosmic sleep on the serpent Ananta ("the Endless"), while the naga king Mucalinda shields Buddha during his many weeks of meditation, protecting him from the rain. Pashupatinath, an avatar of Shiva, is lord of all creatures and is depicted entwined with serpents—the serpent Vasuki is coiled around his neck—and adorned with serpentine armbands. Legend has it that after his marriage to Parvati, these transformed into tattoos. The serpent is closely associated with the creator god, and in the Hebrew scriptures a serpent guards the Tree of Knowledge. Nagas are symbols of the divine consciousness inherent in matter. One of the most powerful symbols of consciousness is the sun (naga can also signify sun).

Nagas as guardians of thresholds

Traditionally, nagas guard doors and thresholds, places of transition—every transition is a change of consciousness. A naga mask is worn in the death ritual (*tiwah*) in the Indonesian province of Kalimantan Tengah. During the dance of death, the coffin lid is raised to reveal the deceased lying on a representation of the naga, with the head of the naga at the feet of the deceased and the tail at the deceased's head, so that the naga becomes a psychopomp (guide) escorting the soul into the realm of the ancestors. The consciousness of the Earth serves as, and indeed embodies, this dimension of the ancestors.

Nagas as vital energy

Life and death are not polar opposites but instead derive from the same source. The naga is not merely an escort into the great beyond but also a bringer of fertility, indeed of the life force itself, of prana. In Hindu tradition, the serpent king Vasuki helped the gods create *amrita*, the elixir of life. As a five-headed serpent, the naga symbolizes the five senses and the "elements" (*tattvas*), although it also represents the *quinta essentia*, the fifth element ether (after earth, water, fire, and air). Its hissing represents the five pranas. The five heads (as the primal element) are therefore also considered the *tanmatras*, the five subtle elements. In this instance, *tan* is mother and *matra* substance or matter. The five forces are simultaneously Mother Earth herself. Consciousness is born from the womb of the Earth, permeating the physicality of Nature (mountains, rivers, lakes, and trees) and rising as a force of consciousness. All this is naga!

Last but not least, naga can also mean lead, one of the densest of the elements. The naga is sun (gold) and Earth (lead) in one being. It is the consciousness of matter and the *quinta essentia* of the philosopher's stone, the mythic substance capable of turning base metals into gold or silver.

We can see that the serpent is closely connected with the creation myth and life on Earth, becoming a symbol of evil (particularly in Christianity) only when the patriarchal religions turned away from sensuality, sexuality, and the Earth itself. It becomes our "shadow" in the Jungian sense, containing all that has been repressed, and as such seems to turn against us. And so male gods and heroes battle the serpent and the dragon as symbols of chaos, or indeed evil: Yahweh defeats Rahab, the Leviathan; Heracles defeats the Hydra and Ladon; Thor, the Midgard Serpent; Ra triumphs over Apopis; and Apollo kills Python.

The Woman and the Serpent

We have seen how in Asia the serpent is regarded as a symbol that is intimately connected with the Earth, and therefore with matter, but also with its polar opposite, the spirit. The serpent is life force and creative urge.

Compare the two myths that follow.

Once upon a time, a young woman was walking in a forest when she met a serpent. "Come!" said the serpent, but the young woman declined, saying, "Who would marry you? You're a serpent. I don't want you." But the serpent replied, "My body may be that of a serpent, but my language is human. Come!" The young woman accepted, married the serpent-man, and bore him a baby girl and boy. The serpent later sent her away with the words: "Go! I shall look after the children and give them something to eat."

The serpent fed the children and they grew up. One day, the serpent said, "Go and catch fish!" and they did. Then the serpent said, "Cook the fish!" However, the children replied, "The sun hasn't come up yet." They waited until sunrise, until the sun had warmed the fish with its rays. Then they ate the raw and bloody fish.

The serpent said, "You are two devils! You eat your food raw. You might eat me. You, boy, get in my belly!" The boy was scared and asked, "What am I supposed to do?" The serpent-man told him to come and the boy entered its belly. Then the serpent said, "Take the fire and bring it out to your sister! Come out, collect coconuts, yams, taro, and bananas!" The boy emerged from the belly, bringing fire with him, and they cooked their food.

This myth is from the Admiralty Islands off the north coast of New Guinea, and we can already see the close connection with dragons in the image of fire in the serpent's belly.

Another well-known story goes as follows.

Now the serpent was more subtil than any beast of the field which the LORD God had made. And he said unto the woman, Yea, hath God said, Ye shall not eat of every tree of the garden? And the woman said unto the serpent, We may eat of the fruit of the trees of the garden: But of the fruit of the tree which is in the midst of the garden, God hath said, Ye shall not eat of it,

Fig. 2. Eve and the serpent portrayed
on the façade of Orvieto Cathedral, Umbria, Italy.

neither shall ye touch it, lest ye die. And the serpent said unto the woman, Ye shall not surely die: For God doth know that in the day ye eat thereof, then your eyes shall be opened, and ye shall be as gods, knowing good and evil.

And when the woman saw that the tree was good for food, and that it was pleasant to the eyes, and a tree to be desired to make one wise, she took of the fruit thereof, and did eat, and gave also unto her husband with her; and he did eat. And the eyes of them both were opened, and they knew that they were naked; and they sewed fig leaves together, and made themselves aprons. And they heard the voice of the LORD God walking in the garden in the cool of the day: and Adam and his wife hid themselves from the presence of the LORD God amongst the trees of the garden. And the LORD God called unto Adam, and said unto him, Where art thou? And he said, I heard thy voice in the garden, and I was afraid, because I was naked; and I hid myself. And he said, Who told thee that thou wast naked? Hast thou eaten of the tree, whereof I commanded thee that thou shouldest not eat? And the man said, The woman whom thou gavest to be with me, she gave me of the tree, and I did eat. And the LORD God said unto the woman, What is this that thou hast done? And the woman said, The serpent beguiled me, and I did eat. (. . .)

Therefore the LORD God sent him forth from the garden of Eden, to till the ground from whence he was taken. So he drove out the man; and he placed at the east of the garden of Eden Cherubims, and a flaming sword which turned every way, to keep the way of the tree of life.

King James version of the Bible, Genesis 3:1–12, 23–24

Although the two accounts come from wholly different cultures, parts of the world, and eras, they are surprisingly similar. From a purely objective point of view, it is the connection between the woman and the serpent that brings consciousness to humanity. In both instances, it is linked to dietary prohibitions and/or commandments. In one case, the serpent brings knowledge, and in the other, fire, but in both, the human only becomes truly human through the actions connected with the serpent.

The Legend of the White Snake is a comparable Chinese myth, in which, after a thousand years of ascetic practice, a white snake transforms itself into a woman called Suzhen who marries a herbalist and healer. In the ancient Chinese myth of Nuwa and Fuxi (legendary rulers), however, we encounter this primordial pair endowed with serpent tails.

Statuettes of women with open bodices and holding snakes in both hands have been discovered in Crete's Palace of Knossos, and the mother goddess Asherah was worshiped by the Canaanites. She too was depicted with serpents and forms a link to Mary, the Mother of God, who is frequently shown standing on and crushing a serpent. Eve is also a mother—her name is derived from *hawwa* (mother of all life), which was also the Semitic word for serpent, making mother and serpent one. In Greek myth, Gaia unites with Uranus (the sky) and gives birth to, among others, the Erinyes (Greco-Roman goddesses of vengeance) who are frequently shown carrying serpents upon their heads; Gaia later also gives birth to Typhon, a giant serpent. The ruler of the Erinyes is Hecate, who, according to the ancient Greek poet

Hesiod, commands the sky, the Earth, and the underworld, in other words, the three worlds of shamanism (the Upper, Middle, and Lower Worlds). She too is depicted in serpent form.

In the ancient Greek Sabazios cult (similar to the Dionysos cult), women would have a snake passed across their vulva in a ritual, the serpent being considered the creative force of Nature itself. Even during his lifetime, a story circulated that Alexander the Great was the child of a human mother and a serpent father.

Around the globe, the snake or serpent is the great bringer of consciousness; as the messenger of the Great God, or as a goddess in its own right, it contributes to the process of becoming human. The woman, the primordial mother, serves as its partner. She receives the life force of the serpent, the ruler of the three worlds.

The Bird and the Serpent

The undertones of the serpent's strong chthonic relationship with the Earth are revealed above all through a symbol that is its opposite, the bird.

The bird and the serpent occur as diametrically opposed symbols in countless myths and visual representations; an eagle fighting a serpent is depicted on Mexico's national coat of arms, for example. Legend has it that, in the form of an eagle, the god Huitzilopochtli led the Aztecs to a new place to settle. At the place where Tenochtitlan, the capital of the new empire, was to be located, the eagle killed a serpent and ate it on a prickly pear, an indigenous myth that has been preserved to this day and is still depicted in various ways, including on Mexican coinage.

Fig. 3. The bird and the serpent as depicted on a Mexican centavo coin.

These two polar forces are engaged in a ubiquitous exchange. The bird, usually an eagle, represents the spiritual or cosmic (Uranian) plane, while the serpent stands for the underworld and the earth-bound, and therefore the life force itself. The shamanic principle of polar forces is so fundamental that the myth occurs on a global level, the only difference being which of the two animals serves as a role model. Zhang Sanfeng, the legendary inventor of t'ai chi ch'üan, is said to have been a Taoist monk and once observed a fight between a bird and a serpent. Whenever the bird pecked with its beak, the serpent gently retreated and the bird was unable to harm it. The serpent became an object lesson for the martial art of t'ai chi ch'üan, in accordance with Taoist beliefs.

In the *Edda* (ancient Norse literature), the serpent/dragon Nidhogg ("the worm of envy") lies at the roots of Yggdrasil, the World Tree, opposite the eagle seated in its crown. The cosmic and the chthonic belong together on the *axis mundi*, the axis of world.

In Indian mythology, the two are fused together as Shesha and Garuda in the form of the "endless serpent," a bird-like hybrid. In ancient Egypt, the vulture of Upper Egypt and the cobra of Lower Egypt are united in the symbolism used by the pharaoh as lord of both worlds, Upper and Lower Egypt, but also of the cosmos and the Earth. The Greek god Hermes is shown with the wings of a bird on his helmet and sandals, and serpents on his staff. With a connection to both the cosmos and Earth, he leads the soul through these realms, fulfilling the role of a shaman as spirit guide. As Hermes Trismegistus,

Fig. 4a. Hermes Trismegistus

Fig. 4b. The caduceus

17

he represents magic: those who unite bird and serpent within themselves become masters of mind and matter. In Hermes' winged, serpent-entwined staff (caduceus), this sorcery becomes a holistic symbol of the magical power inherent in humans: serpent, bird wing, and *axis mundi*. It is part of the perverse nature of human greed that, of all the symbols used in the world, this staff now symbolizes "free trade" and has become one of the basic symbols of capitalism.

It is only in Christianity that the eagle is considered "good" and the snake "evil." More fundamental is the embracing of these two opposing forces in our lives. This essential "dance" can be experienced in shamanic journeys and trances. For Canadian author and anthropologist Jeremy Narby, the DNA ladder and the "cosmic serpent" encountered in experiences induced by the psychoactive South American drink ayahuasca is a mythical mirroring of our DNA: spirit and substance in our essential, basic structure.

The Tale of the White Snake

Fairy tales are mythical stories with deep symbolism, featuring motifs drawn from our rich heritage of cultural and spiritual experiences. Many of these spiritual experiences delve deeply into the fundamental relationship between Earth and humanity. I examined the mythological roots of the Brothers Grimm's stories in my book exploring fairy tales as a mythological bridge to a new consciousness. *The White Snake*, featured in *Grimm's Fairy Tales*, sums up the symbolism and power of the serpent very well. In the end, it is the serpent's power that reconnects humanity and the Earth.

The White Snake
A long time ago, there lived a king whose wisdom was famed throughout the land. There was nothing of which he did not know, and it seemed as if news of even the most obscure things was brought to him through the air. He had a strange custom, however; at midday, when everything had been cleared from

the table and no one else was present, a trusted servant had to bring a further dish. It was covered, however, and not even the servant knew what was inside; no one knew, as the king would only uncover it and eat what was inside when he was completely alone. This went on for a long time until one day, as the servant was carrying the dish away again, he was overcome with curiosity and could not resist. He took the dish to his room and, having carefully locked the door, he lifted the lid and saw that there was a white snake inside. Seeing it, he could not resist the temptation to taste it, so he cut off a small piece and placed it in his mouth. No sooner had it touched his tongue than he heard strange whispering from his window. He went over and listened intently, and noticed that it was the sparrows talking to one another and telling each other of all the things they had seen in the fields and forests. Eating the serpent had given him the ability to understand the language of animals.

It then so happened that this was the day the queen lost her most beautiful ring and the trusted servant, who had access to every part of the palace, was suspected of stealing it. The king called him into his presence and, with mighty curses, threatened that he would be arraigned and condemned for this crime unless he could name the culprit by the following day. Protesting his innocence was useless, and the servant was dismissed without a second bidding. Troubled and scared, he went down to the courtyard and thought about how he could escape his difficult situation. The ducks happened to be peacefully resting side-by-side on a flowing stream, preening themselves with their beaks and having a private conversation. The servant stood still and listened to them. They were talking about all the places they had waddled that morning and how good the food was that they had found. Then one of them said, fretfully, "I have something stuck in my stomach. In my haste, I also swallowed a ring that was under the queen's window." The servant then immediately seized the duck by the neck, carried it into the kitchen, telling the cook, "Slaughter this one, it is well fed."

"Yes," said the cook, weighing it in his hand. "This one hasn't missed any opportunity to fatten itself up, and has been waiting to be roasted for some time." He slit its throat and, when the duck was plucked and drawn, the queen's ring was found in its stomach. The servant was now easily able to prove his innocence to the king and, when the latter wished to make it up to him, he allowed the servant to ask for any favor, promising him the greatest place of honor he might wish for at court.

The servant refused everything and asked only for a horse and some travel money, as he wished to see the world and journey through it for a while. When his wish was granted, he set off and one day, passed a pond in which he noticed three fish that had got trapped in a pipe and were gasping for water. Although it is said that fish cannot speak, he heard them cry out about having to die in such a wretched manner. As he had a compassionate heart, he got down from his horse and returned the three captives to the water. They wriggled in joy, poking their heads out of the water and calling out to him, "We shall remember you and repay you for saving us!" He rode on and, after a while, it seemed as if he could hear a voice coming from the sand at his feet. He listened carefully and was able to make out the king of the ants complaining. "If only people and their clumsy animals would stay away from us! That stupid horse with its heavy hooves is mercilessly trampling my people!" He steered onto a side path and the king of the ants called out to him, "We shall remember you and repay you!" The path took him into a forest, where he saw a mother and father raven standing by their nest and throwing out their young. "Out you get, you scoundrels!" they cried. "We can't satisfy your hunger any more, you are big enough, you can feed yourselves." The poor baby birds lay on the ground, flapping their wings and crying, "We are helpless children and we are supposed to feed ourselves when we can't even fly yet! What else can we do but die of hunger here!" The decent young man then dismounted, killed his horse with his dagger, and left the young ravens some food.

They hopped up, ate their fill, and cried out, "We shall remember you and repay you!"

He now had to go on foot, and after walking a great distance he reached a large city. There was a large, noisy crowd in the street, and then a rider came to announce that the king's daughter was seeking a husband, and anyone who sought her hand would have to complete a great task, and if he could not do it successfully, he would pay with his life. Many had already tried and had gambled with their lives in vain. Seeing the king's daughter, the young man was so dazzled by her beauty that he forgot all the danger and presented himself to the king as a suitor.

He was taken directly to the sea and, before his very eyes, a golden ring was thrown into the water. The king then commanded him to fetch the ring from the bottom of the sea, adding, "If you come back up without it, you will be ducked back in repeatedly until you die in the waves." Everyone then felt sorry for the handsome young man and left him alone beside the sea. Standing on the shore wondering what to do, he saw three fish swimming along, and realized that they were none other than those whose lives he had saved. The middle fish had a mussel in its mouth and placed this on the beach at the young man's feet. He picked it up, opened it, and found the gold ring inside. Full of joy, he brought it to the king, expecting the promised reward to be granted to him. However, when the king's proud daughter saw that he was not of equal birth to her, she shunned him and demanded he complete a second task. She went down into the garden and with her own hands scattered ten sacks of millet onto the lawn. "He must have picked up every one of these before the sun rises tomorrow," she said. "And not a single grain can be missing." The young man sat down in the garden and considered how to complete the task, but he could think of no solution. Deeply saddened, he sat and waited for daybreak when he would be led to his death. But when the first rays of the sun hit the garden, he saw the ten sacks standing in a row, filled to the brim, with not a single grain missing. The king *of the ants had come in the night with his many thousands of ants, and the grateful animals had diligently picked up the millet and collected it in the sacks. The king's daughter came down into the garden herself and saw with amazement that the young man had completed the task he had been set, but she was still unable to restrain her proud heart, and she said, "Even though he has completed both tasks, he shall not be my husband until he has brought me an apple from the Tree of Life." The young man had no idea where the Tree of Life might be so he set off, intending to walk for as long as his legs would carry him, although he had no hope of finding it. When he had walked through three kingdoms and, toward evening, reached a forest, he settled under a tree and hoped to sleep. Suddenly, he heard a noise in the branches and a golden apple fell into his hand. At the same time, three ravens flew down to him, sat on his knee, and said, "We are the three young ravens you saved from death by starvation. When we grew up and heard that you were looking for the golden apple, we flew across the sea to the end of the world where the Tree of Life stands, and fetched you the apple." Full of joy, the young man set off for home and brought the king's beautiful daughter the golden apple. She now had no more excuses left. They shared the apple from the Tree of Life and ate it together. Her heart was then filled with love for him and they lived happily ever after.*

Much like the fairy tale *The Devil with the Three Golden Hairs*, also collected by the Brothers Grimm, which I interpret in my own book about fairy tales, the story of the white snake has a characteristic shamanic structure: a young man works as a servant to a king. In secret, the king has a mysterious dish brought to him daily under cover. Overcome by curiosity, the servant investigates and discovers a white snake that the king eats every day. The servant tries it too and, from that moment on, can understand the language of animals.

The motif of someone eating a snake or dragon, after which they can understand the speech of animals, is an ancient one. In the Icelandic

Volsünga saga (*The Saga of the Volsungs*), the hero Sigurd (*Sigurð*) eats the dragon's heart and can suddenly understand the language of birds, while in Greek mythology, the soothsayer Melampus can comprehend birds after a serpent licks his ears clean. There is also a Serbian fairy tale in which a serpent spits into a young man's mouth, whereupon he too has the power to understand animals.

The serpent is the Great Primordial Serpent, the consciousness of the Earth itself. People have reported being in contact with this serpent after taking the psychoactive drink ayahuasca. In India, as already discussed, snakes are revered as nagas, holy, godlike beings. Traditionally, they guard doors and thresholds, places of transition. Thus, eating the white snake brings people to the threshold of consciousness. Returning to the fairy tale, the servant connects with the consciousness of the Earth and henceforth becomes a shaman, able to understand the speech of animals.

The motif of the ring also reinforces the servant's connection with the Earth. He is suspected of stealing the queen's ring, but thanks to his new ability to understand animals, he recognizes that it has mistakenly been eaten by a bird (a duck or, in another version, a goose), and accordingly the ring is found in the bird's stomach. As a symbol of empathy and partnership, of the "sanctity of marriage," the ring once again demonstrates the connection of the young shaman to animals and to the Earth itself. This is made clear in the version of the tale with the goose; just as in *The Golden Goose* in *Grimm's Fairy Tales,* the goose is an attribute of the Earth: of the Egyptian Earth god Geb, the goddess Nemesis (the protector of Nature), or of the Germanic goddess Hulda. The ring in the stomach of the goose represents the inner connection to the Earth and as such is a soul contract.

The servant then embarks upon his (shamanic) journey. He encounters three fish trapped in a pipe and frees them in accordance with his soul contract with the consciousness of the Earth. He meets a colony of ants and almost tramples many of them to death with his horse, but he understands their warning cries and manages to save them from harm. Finally, he comes across three young ravens that are not yet fledged and in danger of starvation. He sacrifices his steed and uses it to feed the ravens. In Norse mythology, these are the two ravens Hugin and Munin (representing thinking and remembering), who follow Odin as his spirit companions and fly to the ends of the Earth for him.

The servant (of the Earth) fulfils his soul contracts for creatures that live in the earth (ants), in the water (fish), and in the air (ravens). Body (earth), soul (water), and mind (air) are permeated by the consciousness of the Earth as the animals become his soul companions, his power animals. From that point on, these animals, and therefore their own planes of being, serve the servant.

The servant has to complete three tasks in order to achieve royal status and become a perfect human being or a fully fledged shaman: fetch a ring from the seabed, pick up millet from the ground, and bring an apple from the Tree of Life. This is where the three worlds of the shamanic World Tree appear: by fetching the ring from the bottom of the sea with the aid of his power animals (the fish), he penetrates the Lower World and connects (ring symbol) with this sphere of consciousness. The ants help him to pick up food (millet) in the Middle World. He is therefore able to fulfil the demands of physical existence and help to feed his people.

Finally, the ravens fly to the end of the world for the servant (of the Earth), as they do for Odin, and bring him an apple from the Tree of Life. In shamanic terms, they have traveled to the Upper World, the world of paradise. The Tree of Life stands at the (upper) end of the world and at the same time it is also a symbol of the original source of creation. The servant therefore proves that, with the aid of his power animals, he can travel in the Three Worlds.

The story of the white serpent or snake is a great founding myth that takes us back to the sources of our connection to the Earth and the ability of our ancestors to travel in the Three Worlds and so become servants of and companions to the world itself. It is an ability that we still possess today, if we are ready to connect with the Earth.

The pivotal point is the eponymous white snake of the fairy tale, which apparently provides never-ending sustenance in the form of flesh from its body. Should the serpent be interpreted, as elsewhere, as the substance of the Earth, endlessly producing nourishment? However, it is not merely a physical presence but also a provider of a form of knowledge and connection to the Earth. The serpent carries the power of consciousness within it and becomes the path of the shaman, in other words, the path toward becoming a "new human being." It is the serpent and the power that it grants that enable human beings to travel to the Lower, Middle, and Upper Worlds and therefore the World Tree, the *axis mundi*.

We also encounter this trinity of worlds in the Nordic myths. The dragon Nidhogg lives between the roots of the World Tree, a myth we will examine in greater detail later. In the Germanic poem *Völuspá*, Nidhogg drinks the blood of oathbreakers and murderers at the *Náströnd* (shore of corpses) during the "end times," while in the Snorri poem in *The Prose Edda*, Nidhogg remains in the waters of Hvergelmir where he tortures the dead. The "worm of envy" can thus in a way be attributed to the Lower World and therefore to the world of the ancestors.

The Midgard Serpent (*Miðgarðsormr*), on the other hand, is the gigantic World Serpent (*Jörmungandr*, the "vast serpent"), encircling Midgard, the Middle World. When it awakens, space and time (in other words, our reality) will shatter.

In contrast, the eagle lives in the boughs of Yggdrasil, the World Tree. In the *Völuspá* myth, the god Odin, who actually lives in Asgard in the Upper World, transforms himself into both a serpent and an eagle, so eagle and serpent become one in him.

The serpent is ultimately present in all three shamanic worlds and is master of them, hence its ability in the tale of the white snake to lead the hero through all the worlds. In its symbolism, the serpent is considerably more than "just" the physical Earth; it is more like existence itself, encompassing the physical and non-physical.

The Meaning of
the Dragon

The winged serpent as a link between the bird, a creature of the air, and the serpent, a creature of the Earth, should be seen as a step on the path to the symbol of the dragon. As we have already seen, the serpent and dragon are similar in their essence, so we will now focus on the dragon and its literal meaning, since it reveals much about the symbolic and mythological significance of this creature with its very close connection to the Earth.

The English word "dragon" is derived from the Latin *draco*. Other terms are related to lindwyrm (see opposite) and are found in Swedish, Old Danish, Old High German, Icelandic, and throughout Central Europe.

The Latin term *draco* is derived in turn from the Greek *drákōn*, which has the modern sense of dragon but can also mean serpent. This double association with dragon and serpent frequently crops up both in symbolism and in related terms such as wyvern (see opposite), and is essential to the meaning of "dragon." So the dragon, like the serpent, is always earth-related, even when venerated as an air dragon in China; the element of air (and also, by analogy, the element of water with water dragons) should be understood as one of the elements associated with the Earth (as a planet or mythologically as a goddess).

The Greek δράκων, *drákōn*, comes in turn from δέρκεσθαι, *dérkesthai*, which means "to see." Extended meanings of the latter include: to look at, regard, glimpse, perceive, focus on, or even to shed light on. *Drákōn* can therefore be freely translated as "the animal that sees, that perceives." Clearly, dragon is derived from, or strongly influenced by, the symbolism of sight and the eye.

The eye is also a symbol of insight, indeed of enlightenment, or in other words, of spiritual growth. The Greek philosopher Plato maintains that the eye is the human sensory organ that most closely resembles the sun, embodying brightness, light, clairvoyance, and spirit.

All this is inherent in a dragon; it is understood as a being that promotes humanity's understanding and as a spirit that perceives on behalf of the Earth. Just like the sun, which represents the eye, the dragon is a symbol of divinity while simultaneously being an instrument of the Earth.

The term "lindwyrm," which was more common in some Germanic languages into the 9th century, once again emphasizes the serpent symbolism of dragons. *Linnormr* was a tautological compound of two nouns with the same meaning *linni* (serpent), related to *lindi* (soft, gentle, yielding, pliable), and *orm* (worm). A lindwyrm was a wriggling worm. Interestingly, legend also attributes powerful vision to the lindwyrm and, much like another variant the basilisk, the lindwyrm is able to hypnotize, paralyze, or even to kill with just a glance. It is said a lindwyrm once lived in the so-called *Spiegelbrunnen* (mirror well) in Munich, Germany, and killed anyone who looked down into the well, until it was paralyzed by its own reflection in a mirror that was hung above it. The term lindwyrm, which was in common usage before the word dragon, consequently also has the same symbolism as the dragon in terms of the all-seeing, all-knowing eye.

In the German language, the expression *Tatzelwurm*, combining *Tatze* (paw) and *Wurm* (worm), describes a dragon/serpent equipped with feet. Wyverns, however, are generally depicted as dragon-like creatures whose front limbs have formed into wings (much like birds). The term comes from the 13th-century English word *wyver*, which in turn is derived from Old French *wivre* and French *vouivre*, and is related to the Latin word *vipera* (viper). Interestingly, *vouivre* (*wyver*) is also related to the French word *vivre* (live), as is the Latin *vipera*, which derives from *vivipar* (giving live birth). We therefore encounter the winged serpent, the wyvern, in particular as a symbol of life force.

27

The Dragon as a Bringer of Culture

The dragon as a symbol of disaster and evil is widespread in Christian legend, especially in patriarchal cultures. In other, generally much older, myths, the dragon appears not only as the source of vital energy but also as the force that brings culture *per se* to humankind, as described in the legend from New Guinea (see page 13).

The origin myths of some Asian peoples refer to their legendary ancient rulers and bearers of culture as being descended from dragons. Lạc Long Quân, which translates as the "dragon ruler of Lạc," is the mythological founder of Vietnam and the bringer of culture to the Vietnamese people. His father was Shennong, who once married the daughter of the dragon Thần Long Nữ, so Lạc Long Quân was literally a "dragon's son." Lạc Long Quân married the mountain goddess Âu Cơ. We can see in this union the intimate interconnectedness of the early rulers with the land and upon which their wisdom, knowledge, and supremacy was based. Lạc Long Quân taught his people fishing, rice cultivation, and cooking, as well as the art of tattooing.

Lạc Long Quân's Chinese equivalent is Fuxi, who taught humankind much, including how to catch fish using a net, animal husbandry by taming wild beasts, and the breeding of silkworms. Some legends also attribute the arts of kindling fire and tool-making to him, as well as the measurement of time and space (using knotted cord). The Chinese geomantic practice of feng shui can also ultimately be traced back in mythology to Fuxi. He was the eighth son (dragon son) of his ancestor the Ancient Dragon Mother Tsin-Kong. Like his wife Nuwa, Fuxi is depicted as half human, half dragon. So the bearer of culture received wisdom and the knowledge that he passed on to humanity directly from a dragon.

The dragon is closely related to the first cultural heroes. In India, Shiva (as his avatar Pashupatinath) is the lord of all creatures and is depicted entwined with serpents and dragons. The naga serpent, seen here as the source of his power, is also a symbol of the divine consciousness inherent in matter, bringing fertility and prana, or life force.

Fig. 5. The legend of Faridun
as depicted in an Islamic book illustration.

In Persia, the first ruler Faridun, who is said to have lived at the dawn of Persian history, had three sons. In order to determine which of them should succeed him, Faridun transformed himself into a dragon. He decreed that the son who stood up to the dragon without fleeing, yet who also refrained from killing it, would be the one to be crowned king.

Even Heustero, the Indo-Germanic goddess of the hearth fire, took her power from the "serpent of the hearth." Fire was intimately associated with dragons at the dawn of our culture—not just the physical fire that enabled us to cook food, but also, importantly, the intellectual, spiritual fire brought by the dragon. For the Aztecs and Toltecs, it was the winged serpent/dragon Quetzalcoatl that created humankind from maize and ground gemstones.

And what about Europe? Along with countless dragon-slaying legends, the power of the dragon as the source of human culture at the dawn of time can be found in several ancient myths. Delphi was the home of the (initially female) dragon (or snake) Python, son of the primordial mother Gaia, the Earth itself. According to the *Homeric Hymns,* Python was born from primeval slime and has been present since the beginning of life on Earth. As dragons have watched over evolution and life on Earth since the earliest times, in legends they are frequently the guardians of treasure, not from greed but a sense of stewardship. The Slavic god Svarožić, also known as Dažbog or Radegast, was a sun and fire god and the divine father of the Slavic pantheon. He too would occasionally appear in the form of a mighty dragon. He was a god of light but also of fire, which he gave to humans as a gift. As such, he was greatly revered as a bringer of life.

The power of dragons as bringers of life and culture is also deeply rooted in Celtic myths—the leading chieftain of the Celts was known as Pendragon (head dragon). In Arthurian myth, Arthur's father is called Uther Pendragon, so the power of the country's dragon was referenced in the Celtic princes. In Gwynedd in Wales (a country that has a red dragon on its national flag, see page 49), purported sightings persist of a dragon near the burial site of the Welsh tribal prince Ederyn. Again, the dragons are not evil but could become angry if they perceive that people are taking without giving, such as in taking possession of land without showing the dragon (and therefore the power of the dragon) the necessary respect. The Earth will then begin to quake, floods will rise, and fire will destroy forests and harvests. A mirror for our current times, perhaps?

Dragons were considered real creatures by some well into the 19th century. The German entomologist Samuel Schilling devoted a chapter to dragons in his 1837 encyclopedic work on the animal, vegetable, and mineral kingdoms (*Ausführliche Naturgeschichte des Thier-, Pflanzen- und Mineralreichs*): "When all the various tales about mythical dragons are compared, a living creature does indeed seem to have given rise to these narratives, and this animal was without doubt none other than the great boa constrictor, which lives in India and Africa and can grow to a length of 30 to 40 feet."

As the elemental source of Earth's life force and a spiritual stimulus of human history, dragons are also closely linked with the foundation myths of numerous cities, including Basel (see page 58), Klagenfurt, Murnau, Krakow, and the City of London, where the dragon has been an emblem of the city since the 14th century. It has featured on its coat of arms since the 17th century and appears on boundary markers on points of entry into the Square Mile, as the heart of the city is known. However, with the patriarchal world view of these stories, instead of being grateful for what these dragons could bring, they became creatures to be fought or slain as people claimed the fertility of the Earth as their own.

The Chinese Dragon

In European cultures, as society became more patriarchal and with Christianization, the dragon increasingly became a symbol of fear and evil. This was at odds, however, with the use of the dragon in geomancy. Here, the dragon is a symbol of primeval power and is deeply connected with the landscape—indeed with the life and creative power of the Earth itself, with mountains, water, and so on. In this respect, the image of the dragon in geomancy is more akin to that of the dragon in Chinese mythology.

In Chinese mythology, the dragon (*long/lung*) is a spiritual, even divine being. As such, dragons are first documented in China as a

Fig. 6. Chinese dragon, Fayu Temple, China.

mythical expression of a benevolent elemental force in around 400 BCE. Their divinity is revealed in Chinese folklore in the legendary ancient ruling couple Fuxi and Nuwa (see page opposite), who were children of a dragon, and in Ao Guang, the Dragon King of the East Sea. We will take a closer look at Fuxi and his wife in due course.

The Chinese dragon often features in a water setting, such as in rivers, lakes, ocean bays, and sometimes in springs. When said to dwell in mountains, it is often associated with the rain clouds that bring fertility. The writhing, serpent-like Chinese dragon, which appears to swim rather than fly through the air, is therefore symbolically linked with the so-called "primeval waters."

The Chinese dragon is not restricted in its form, however. A Chinese proverb says that the dragon has nine sons, each one different. The equally auspicious symbols of the tortoise and lion are therefore viewed in China as variants of the dragon. Dragons can even transform into human beings, an expression of how the dragon power of the Earth is inherent in every animal, including people. The primeval power of the dragon is what gives the natural world—the animal and vegetable kingdoms—its life force, and for humans, it results in a long life, happiness, prosperity, and contentment.

Discussions of dragons in this context refer specifically to the force that is associated with what is known as "soul water" (see page 74) and is the primal cause of the creative power of life. In turning away from this force, with the spread of the patriarchy, people began to subjugate Nature instead of working with it and for it, exploiting Nature rather than promoting it, using and abusing animals rather than protecting them, and employing the primeval forces of the Earth for humankind's own technological ends. This attitude finds symbolic expression in the slaying of dragons and fear of the elemental forces of life.

We live in a time of change in which it will be necessary to fundamentally rethink our relationship with dragons if the ongoing survival of human beings is to be guaranteed. We must set dragons free rather than slay them. We must rediscover the dragon within us.

The Legacy of the Dragon

To get to the roots of geomantic systems and ways of thinking, we cannot avoid encountering mythical figures. One such is the "ancestor" of humanity (from a Chinese perspective), Fuxi, China's legendary first emperor, whom we have encountered as a bringer of culture. He is one of the mythical figures behind China's cultural beginnings.

Fuxi is revered for a whole series of concepts and teachings specific to the spiritual comprehension of Nature and the Earth in geomancy and/or feng shui:

- the concept of yin and yang,
- the Four Symbols (*si xiang*),
- the principle of the eight trigrams (particularly in their so-called "early heaven" sequence).

The mythical ruler

The story of Fuxi, the legendary first emperor of China, begins even before his birth. The Ancient Dragon Mother Tsin-Kong is an ancient Taoist myth— women in particular would seek refuge with her when giving birth to their children. Nine legendary "dragon sons" (rulers) can be traced back to Tsin-Kong, including Fuxi, the eighth son. In another version of the story, it was the demigod ruler Nuwa who created humanity at the beginning of history; she is depicted as a human with a dragon's body and is a vestige of China's early

Fig. 7. The legendary Chinese rulers Fuxi and Nuwa with the bodies of serpents.

matriarchal society. Fuxi and Nuwa are often represented together as the first ruling couple. The emperor receives his authority as a descendant of the ancient dragon mother, hence often being referred to as the dragon son. In this way, female power was transferred to the male ruler.

At first Fuxi was the "ruler of heaven." He observed the coloration and structure of the sky, then turned his gaze to the Earth and the colors and markings of birds and other animals, and finally he studied the contours of the ground. In this way, he became aware of the interrelation between the forces of Nature and the way in which everything is suffused with Qi, the "breath" of the Earth and heaven.

Recognizing the laws of the world, Fuxi measured time and space and invented the set square. As soon as order had been brought to the world, Fuxi and his mother/sister Nuwa were united as husband and wife. Fuxi therefore carries a set square as a symbol both of his spiritual and magical powers and of the masculine, whereas Nuwa carries a pair of compasses (with which circles are drawn), the circle being a symbol of the feminine. These are also symbols of geomancy and are used in architecture too, of course.

The Laughing Buddha and the Dragon

In China the Laughing Buddha (布袋 *Bùdài*), anything but ascetic in appearance, represents the more worldly aspect of Chan Buddhism. In Japan this developed into Zen Buddhism. In combination with the Chinese dragon, the Budai is not just a powerful symbol of good fortune, also commonly used in feng shui, but also, and more importantly, the vision of a spiritual future for humanity bound to the Earth.

The Laughing Buddha

In complete contrast to the Indian depiction of a gaunt and introspective Buddha, Budai, known in Japan as Hotei, is depicted pot-bellied and always laughing. According to legend, he was a monk named Qici (契此) from the province of Zhejiang, who lived in the 10th century. Because of his ample proportions, he was nicknamed Bùdài, or "gunnysack." He is said to have spoken with a stutter and would always fall asleep wherever he happened to lie down, characteristic of Parzifal. However, the monk Qici was also highly skilled in magic and had the gift of clairvoyance. He could influence the weather, which meant that snow never settled on him (a symbol of eternal spring), and his close affinity with dragons in this context is already evident. Despite his considerable magical powers, Qici was very modest and always content with whatever morsels of food people gave him. He collected edible donations in his body, so to speak, and non-edible ones in a sack, with which he is often depicted, filled to the brim.

In China the figure of Budai merged with the Indian Maitreya Buddha. Maitreya is often called the Buddha of the Future, as according to legend he dwells in Tushita, one of the heavens of Indian divinities. Godlike, Maitreya is awaiting his rebirth as a bodhisattva, which is due to take place at the end of the current era. Like a messiah figure, Maitreya will then bring enlightenment to all humanity.

Equating Budai with Maitreya might seem paradoxical, but this connection is ubiquitous in East Asia and is based on his preachings; he never tired of explaining that Maitreya is already omnipresent, now, in every person, plant, and animal. Budai was actually preaching

Fig. 8. Buddha and dragon:
enlightenment and connection with the Earth.

enlightenment through Nature and the Earth, and so in Japan the Laughing Buddha is counted as one of the Seven Gods of Fortune (*Shichifukujin*). He reveals a vision in which humans will experience enlightenment in the near future by turning to life in all its profundity and sacredness.

Buddha and the dragon

When a dragon is depicted together with the Milifu Buddha, the origins of the dragon as an all-knowing child of the Earth are fused with the vision of a human being finding their way back to the Earth, thereby achieving enlightenment and creating an idyllic state (the Golden Age) on Earth. Humankind and Earth are reunited in the two beings tenderly entwining. This is a vision of the currently emerging geoculture and the promise that human beings and the Earth will mutually benefit one another.

The Dragon's Hoard

We discussed the dragon as a symbol of prosperity, indeed of wealth, in Asian symbolism in the previous chapter, but in Europe the dragon is also closely linked with vast stores of treasure. We are all familiar with the images common in fables, legends, and fairy tales, or even in fantasy literature, where a dragon guards an unfathomably large trove of treasure, the so-called dragon's hoard. The symbolic connection between dragon and treasure runs so deep that it is difficult to separate them. In the 14th-century Icelandic *Gull-Þóris saga*, the dragon is a hero named Viking Vali, who, with his entire clan of dragons, guards a great store of treasure until he is defeated by Thorir. In the collection of heroic Old Norse narrative poems, *The Poetic Edda*, the dragon Fáfnir (see page 46) also guards such a hoard that he has amassed on the Gnita Heath. In the *Völsunga saga*, Fáfnir's treasure is stored in an otter skin (his slain brother, who would assume the shape of an otter) that had to be filled with gold until no part of it was visible—treasure as a kind of sacrifice in atonement. And in the legendary story of Beowulf, the dragon-like monster Grendel guards a treasure. We could go on. . . .

Much of this treasure is magical, but it is also often cursed. The hoard is so much more than mere treasure promising great wealth. The ring of the Nibelungs has the power to increase the treasure, but it is cursed and brings death to its owner. The treasure symbolizes a gift, a primordial mental and spiritual state that is watched over by the guardian dragon. Since the dragon is closely associated with the Earth (as discussed extensively in other chapters), it dwells in mountains, caves, or underground, where it also stores its treasure; in this way, the dragon's hoard represents the Earth's great treasures.

Thanks to our attitudes, we often view the riches of the Earth as mere raw materials, but they are much greater than this. As frequently related in myths and legends, the riches of the Earth can transform their possessor, and if this treasure is stolen, the new owner can become greedy and violent (just as the Arkenstone, found in the Lonely Mountain, hardens the heart of Thorin Oakenshield in *The Hobbit*). If the treasure is won or given as a gift, however, the new owner is also gifted with all kinds of abilities and generosity of spirit. In this way, the treasure permits the rediscovery of a person's soul relationship with Nature and the Earth. It requires, as fairy tales so delightfully put it, a pure heart, which in itself is a kind of treasure.

In this sense, the dragon's lair is a hidden chamber connecting us with the depths of the soul of the Earth. Finding this chamber in your own heart also opens up the Earth/soul space. For the winning of treasure to be auspicious, the dragon does not need to be conquered but instead to be approached with an open heart and the treasure will be given freely.

The dragon and dwarves

The treasure of dwarves is closely associated with dragon hoards, a connection that is most obvious in Eddic fables such as the *Reginsmál* and *Fáfnismál*. In these Regin is both a dwarf and the brother of Fáfnir the dragon. A brother motif invariably refers to a form of kinship or even identity. Regin is the foster father of Sigurd and is also responsible for forging the dragon-slaying sword Gram. Dragon, dwarf, and dragon's hoard are closely interrelated in their symbolism, forming a kind of symbolic ring. In the Nibelung saga, it is the dwarf Alberich who becomes guardian of the Nibelung treasure.

This close symbolic relationship is a further reminder that the hoard is underground treasure, as the dwarves are intimately connected with the Earth, mountains, and mineshafts. As the influence of Christianity grew, dwarves, once helpful spirits, like the dragons were increasingly depicted as greedy and malevolent.

Buried treasure appears to function as a mirror—whatever a person projects into it is reflected back at them. The more spiritually distanced people are from the planet, the more the helpful spirits of the Earth seem to take the form of malevolent and vengeful dwarves, and the dragons become symbols of absolute evil. The close association of dwarf and dragon makes it clear that the dragon is ultimately also an "Earth spirit," but its essence is more archaic and more primal than that of the dwarves.

The soul mirror

The treasure of the Earth lies buried in the deepest depths underground. It is closely linked with the Earth itself and, as a mirror of the soul, reflects what a person wants to see in the Earth. Stealing it is not an option, there must be a redemption of the treasure, as it were, in a new geocultural relationship between human beings and the Earth. The task is to discover the treasure in order to become the treasure. If humans themselves become the treasure of the Earth, the treasure will be equally available to all and dragons will watch over it.

The Dragon and the Stars

In the last few chapters, we have outlined many aspects of the dragon and the serpent as symbols of rootedness in the Earth, but in folk mythologies both have a counterpart known as a "star dragon" or "celestial serpent."

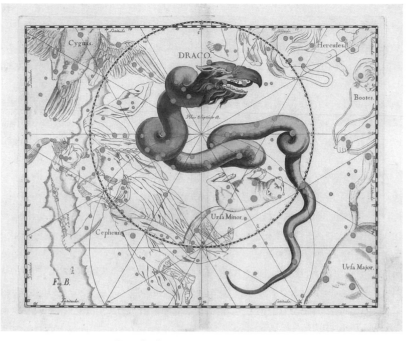

Fig. 9. Constellation of Draco,
as depicted in Johannes Hevelius' *Uranographia*.

It is notable, of course, that the dragon constellation Draco is one of the most powerful in the northern sky. Draco wraps around Ursa Minor, the Little Bear, and is therefore a circumpolar constellation in its own right. In the Ptolemaic system formulated in antiquity, the Little Bear was seen as a wing of the dragon in the Draco constellation. The mighty dragon in the sky is adjacent to eight other constellations, dancing in its rotation around the pole star. Around 5,000 years ago, in the time of ancient Egypt, the principal star Alpha Draconis (α Draconis, Thuban) served as the pole star; in fact, Alpha Draconis is a binary star system in Draco, as has recently been discovered.

In Babylonian mythology, the constellation Draco is one half of the primordial dragon Tiamat that when slain became part of the sky; celestial serpent and earthly snake are as one. In the legend of Heracles, the hero has to defeat the dragon Ladon to reach the apples of the

Hesperides. In this clear reference to paradise, the dragon guards the World Tree with its miraculous apples just as the snake guards the Tree of Knowledge in the Garden of Eden. Ladon was then placed among the stars in the heavens by Hera to form the constellation Draco.

In Chinese astronomy and astrology, the Azure Dragon (Qīng Lóng), which is associated with the East and with spring, is not just a constellation but a whole quadrant of the sky. This "spring palace" includes what in Western astronomy are known as the constellations Virgo, Libra, Scorpio, and Sagittarius.

The Azure Dragon is sometimes amalgamated with the creator goddess Nuwa who, as we have seen, was also depicted in dragon form. As the four pillars holding up the sky began to crumble, a part of the heavens fell in, the Earth tilted toward the southeast and the sky toward the northwest, and the axis of the world was slanted. With the aid of five colored stones (the five phases of transformation), Nuwa patched and mended the sky to save humanity. The Azure Dragon is also sometimes encountered as a rainbow intended to connect this world with the next. We again see the harmony of the Earth dragon Nuwa as a creator goddess with the celestial serpent, both of whom created the pillar holding up the world that is also the bridge into the ancestral world.

In ancient Egypt all these roles are assumed by Kebechet (of the Old Kingdom), the goddess of the dead, who is depicted as a celestial serpent with ostrich feathers. As an "opener of the heavens," Kebechet took care of the deceased's path to the stars. Later, the soul would often be depicted riding a serpent to the stars and was then regarded as a personification of Isis. Here, the sky serpent is opening the way to the ancestral worlds. In Norse mythology too, the Nidhogg dragon flies with the dead at the end of the *Völuspá* saga.

For the Aztecs, the cloud snake Mixcoatl, seen as a manifestation of the Milky Way, performs exactly the same function. Mixcoatl transports the souls of dead warriors to the heavens, where they become stars. It was also Mixcoatl who brought fire to humankind. Physical fire, soul-fire, and the stars are all one.

The celestial serpent and the sky dragon form a bridge between the material world and the spiritual space of the stars, which is why, in the Revelation of St John in the Christian Bible, it is a dragon (once again interpreted as evil) whose tail sweeps a third of the stars from the sky and hurls them to the Earth (at the same time also forging a link between the stars and the Earth).

The earthly serpent and the sky dragon are therefore symbolically connected and in this way link the cosmos and the Earth as a soul path; indeed, they are ultimately the *axis mundi* itself. To this day, the star dragon dances around the cosmic end of the world's axis in the northern sky, inspiring humanity with the fire of the stars.

When Christians Heal Dragons

In Christian symbolism dragons are mostly encountered as motifs of evil, with the dragon (the devil) being defeated and slain by saints such as St George, St Beatus, and St Michael. It is an association so fundamental and deep-rooted that many symbolic interpretations cannot see beyond it.

There are, nonetheless, other, entirely different depictions of dragons in Christianity. Saint Simeon Stylites the Younger lived in the borderlands between Syria and Cilicia during the 6th century. In the year 547, Simeon (also known as Symeon) is said to have climbed the Hill of Wonders and taken up residence on a very high pillar on the site of the present-day monastery. The symbol of the *axis mundi* is echoed in the Christian ascetic, or stylite, who spends his life on a tall pillar (Simeon's pillar is described as being more than 80 feet, or almost 25 meters, high). The World Pillar (Old Saxon, Irminsul) is a connection between heaven and Earth symbolically related to the World Tree. Seated on the top of a pillar, the saint lives out his life in the Upper World, in the crown of the World Tree. Simeon Stylites, who lived in this manner, is said to have descended on only a very few occasions, but one such occasion was in order to heal a dragon!

Fig. 10a. St Simeon Stylites on a pillar with a serpent.

Fig. 10b. St Margaret, Obersaxen, Switzerland.

At that time there dwelt an extraordinarily large dragon nearby [in the vicinity of St Simon Stylites] in the northern regions, where no grass grew; and a stick had got caught in its right eye. And behold, this blind dragon approached the little dwelling where the man of God lived, dragging itself along; it lay there with bowed head, and its body was wrapped around itself in a ring, as it if were asking for a boon. When St Simeon saw this, he immediately removed a huge stick from its eye and when the people saw this, they all praised God and fled from that place in awe. But the animal rolled up into a ball and remained rooted to the spot, unmoving, until all the people had passed by. It then stood up, paid homage to the monastery door for almost two hours, and then returned to its cave, not hurting a soul.

[Vita S. Simeon Stylites (PL 73, 330, 7–24)]

In Fig. 10a, the relationship between humans and dragons (as the symbol of Earth's primeval power) is not portrayed as a brutal struggle but instead as loving and even healing. The dragon appears as a serpent that winds itself about the pillar, just as the snake winds around the Staff of Aesculapius, the symbol of healing.

Other examples of a similar relationship include a legend originating in Poitiers (France) in which yet another battle with a dragon is described, but in this instance people venerate the dragon rather than the knight who slew it. The dragon is revered as *la bonne sainte vermine* (the good and holy monster), the last vestiges of a loving reverence for the elemental powers of the Earth that prevailed in the pre-Christian era.

In Obersaxen, in Switzerland (Fig. 10b), a Gothic winged altarpiece features St Margaret with a dragon, an image that appeals for its tenderness rather than any implied dragon-slaying. We look at the legend of St Margaret and the dragon in more depth on page 81. In another reversal of the relationship, St Eudocia was protected by a dragon that defended her against her persecutors.

It is clear that until the dawn of the Christian era, the relationship between people and dragons was seen in a positive light. Indeed, human beings, dragons, and the Earth are closely connected, as the following chapters reveal.

Gaia and the Dragon

In a striking scene on the portal of St Mark's Basilica in Venice, a partially clad woman is shown sitting on a dragon with leaves sprouting from her hands. The tail of the dragon has formed into a second, smaller dragon that is trying to suckle like a baby at the woman's breast.

Who is this woman? It cannot be the Virgin Mary crushing a serpent, as Christians like to represent her. Many of the features are similar, but the Mother of God is depicted bare-breasted only infrequently and then nursing the infant Christ rather than a dragon, which for Christians generally represents evil. What is the identity of this woman who is so clearly intimately linked with the power of the dragon?

It is in fact Gaia. It is Nature, the Earth itself. She is riding the dragon and nourishing it at the same time, the leaves springing from her hands providing absolute proof of this.

Gaia is astride the dragon, an ancient symbol of the primordial power of the Earth. With the paws of a lion and spitting flames (fire), and with the scales of a fish (water), the body of a reptile (earth), and equipped with wings (air), the dragon unites the four elements of fire, water, earth, and air, and indeed, the fifth element, so to speak, the *quinta essentia*, ether.

This elemental force of the Earth, the life force, is simultaneously nourished and ridden by Gaia. The power of the dragon is the vehicle of life on Earth, permeating sexuality, creativity, the life force of plants, and the breath of animals and human beings alike. Dragon power is the life force on which Gaia's work is founded. This is why she rides the dragon; it is her steed, her vehicle, the means through which she ensures the flow of the processes of life on Earth.

The power of the dragon is at the same time directly nourished by Gaia herself; it suckles at her breast in the same way that Christ is nursed and fed by Mary. The dragon takes in the essence, the being of Gaia, with its mother's milk. In its relationship with Gaia, the dragon is portrayed as an active force of the Great Goddess as well as being intimately connected with her. Whoever disturbs or harms the one, also harms the other. Both are inseparably connected.

If the slaying of a dragon has been elevated to the highest of principles in patriarchal cultures, it goes hand-in-hand with the killing of Nature. The confinement and imprisonment, torture and suppression of the joys of life (song and dance, physical closeness, breath, and fertility) with which we confront Nature, plants, animals, and indeed other human beings too, are an expression of an attempt to conquer the power of the dragon, even to slay the dragon itself. But we overlook the fact that in so doing we are destroying the very basis of our life force, the breath of life, and the water of our soul. Without the dragon, there is no Gaia, and without Gaia, there are no human beings.

This image from Venice is a perpetual reminder, particularly in the current time, not to fight the intimate bond between the dragon and the Earth; instead, we are called upon to respect, to honor, and to support it. The elemental power of the Earth must be allowed to exist freely. Dragon energy that is constrained and restricted will result in human beings who are constrained, suppressed, and drained, robbed of any joy in life and degraded into soulless automata, just as we demean animals into soulless producers of meat and milk in factory farming.

This time has passed. Indeed, it must be over if we are to live on as spiritual creatures.

Gaia and the dragon are one.

Famous Dragons

It is time to take a closer look at some of the best-known dragons and the myths associated with them.

Fáfnir

In Nordic myth, the dragon Fáfnir (or Fefner, literally "the Embracer") is the virtual prototype of a monster guarding treasure. He was originally the son of the dwarf king Hreidmar (*Hreiðmarr*). His brother Ótr, who would assume the form of an otter during the day, was slain and skinned by the gods Loki and Odin while they were out hunting. However, Hreidmar, Fáfnir, and Regin, Fáfnir's second brother, took the gods prisoner and demanded *weregild* (monetary compensation) to atone for Ótr's death. They were to fill the entire otter skin with gold, but the pelt grew larger with every handful of gold placed inside it. As result, Hreidmar amassed a huge fortune. Using blackmail, Loki then extorted treasure from Alberich, lord of the dwarves, which happened to also contain the ring of the Nibelungs. Alberich cursed the ring so that whoever wore it would die a violent death.

Hreidmar slipped on the ring and Fáfnir was overcome by greed for the riches that he saw. He killed his own father in order to have all the gold for himself. This violent deed transformed Fáfnir's appearance and he changed into the dragon guarding the Nibelung treasure.

Regin, Fáfnir's brother, encouraged Sigurd to kill Fáfnir. Sigurd dug a ditch and stabbed Fáfnir with the demonic sword Gram, and the dragon's blood flowed into the ditch. Once Sigurd had tasted the dragon's blood and heart, he was able to understand the language of birds (see *The White Snake* fairy tale, page 18). He then heard that Mime, the blacksmith, wanted to kill him. In one variation of the story, Sigurd bathes in the dragon's blood and becomes invincible, save for a single spot on his back where a heart-shaped linden leaf had fallen and so remained free of blood. The "back of the heart" is therefore a symbol for the eternally vulnerable part of a person, the sensitive inner self.

The dragon Fáfnir embodies the elemental forces of the Earth, however; understanding the language of animals and making flesh invulnerable, he guards the treasures of the Earth. Just as in the Christian Eucharist, in which the blood of Christ transforms those who drink it, the blood of the dragon, a primordial force of the Earth, transforms those whose lips it touches. In Nordic myth, this elemental force has already been corrupted by human greed and so Fáfnir becomes a beast, a monster.

The Hydra

The fertile land of Lerna was under threat from the Hydra, a dragon that lived near the Amymone springs and was destroying crops. It had a multitude of snake heads—between five and a thousand, depending on the source—and when one was cut off, two new heads would grow back in its place.

According to Greek mythology, the Hydra of Lerna was the daughter of the dragon Typhon, whose hundred heads spat fire, and the female dragon Echidna, a snake with a woman's head. Its siblings were the many-headed hellhound Cerberus, the Chimera, and the Sphinx. King Eurystheus asked Heracles to slay the Hydra. Protected from the Hydra's venom by the skin of the Nemean Lion, he tried to kill it by smashing its heads with his club, but the heads grew back in vast numbers. Heracles then fired burning arrows at Hydra to tempt it out of its lair and chopped off its heads with a sword, but this too was to no

Fig. 12. Heracles and Iolaos fighting the Hydra,
Hans Sebald Beham (1545).

avail. In addition, Hera, the jealous mother of the gods (Heracles had been the result of an "adventure" between Zeus and Alcmene) sent a giant crab to attack Heracles' feet.

Heracles realized that he was not able to kill the Hydra alone, so aided by Iolaos, his nephew, he crushed the crab beneath his foot and clubbed off the Hydra's heads while Iolaos cauterized the wounds so that the heads could not grow back. Ultimately, all that remained was the "immortal head" of the Hydra, and when Heracles removed this with a single blow, the dragon finally died.

The constellation Hydra (the water snake) is the longest constellation in the night sky, extending beneath the constellations Cancer (crab), Leo (lion), and Virgo (maiden), and here we can see the mythological link to the skin of the Nemean Lion, worn by Heracles, and the crab that attacks him. The constellation Hercules (Heracles) is the fifth-largest in the northern sky and is found in the proximity of Corona Borealis, the "northern crown." The constellations of Hydra and Hercules are among those described by Ptolemy, an astronomer of Greek descent working in the second century AD; Hydra can be seen just above the southern horizon in spring.

Heracles' battle with the Hydra can also be understood as a hopeless struggle against the rhythms of Nature. However often the Hydra is slain, each spring it will always reappear on the southern horizon.

The Red Dragon of Wales

The national flag of Wales, part of the UK, has featured a red dragon on a white and green field (background) since 1807; the Welsh motto is *Y ddraig goch ddyry cychwyn* (the red dragon leads the way). However, the red dragon of Wales is associated with a legend involving a white dragon.

The story goes that in the mountains of Snowdonia in North Wales, King Vortigern built a castle with a tower as a defensive fortification against the Anglo-Saxons. Unfortunately, the tower collapsed repeatedly no matter how often Vortigern rebuilt it. Soothsayers advised the king to find a fatherless child and anoint the walls with its blood to make the walls more solid. A child was consequently found and brought before the king. According to the 9th-century *Historia Brittonum* (*History of the Britons*), this child was Ambrosius Aurelianus, whose father was said to have been a Roman consul, although the legend also maintains that the child was none other than Merlin, the mythical enchanter and sage associated with King Arthur.

However, the child was wise and decided to try and save his life by telling Vortigern the real reason for the collapse of the tower. The king agreed to listen and Ambrosius/Merlin explained that it was due to the presence of a marsh beneath the castle in which lived two dragons— one red and one white—it was the movements of these beasts that were shaking the walls and causing them to fall. Vortigern ordered the marsh to be drained and the two dragons were indeed discovered, and on waking up, immediately attacked one another.

Ambrosius/Merlin had also made a prophecy: *Woe indeed, the end of the red dragon is nigh! The white dragon that will nest in its cave is revealed as the Anglo-Saxons that King Vortigern brought here. The red dragon represents the people of the Britons, who will defeat the white dragon: for the mountains and valleys of Britain will collapse in on themselves and the streams and rivers will turn to blood.* However, the red dragon would ultimately defeat the white dragon, the child continued.

It is at this point that the legends diverge. The Welsh version maintains that the red dragon, which represents the Celtic Britons, ultimately defeats the white dragon, which is why the red dragon features on the Welsh national flag, representing courage and perseverance. However, other myths make connections with Arthurian legend. In these the white dragon destroys the red dragon when King Vortigern, portrayed as a usurper, seizes the throne from the true king of the Britons, Uther Pendragon (the father of Arthur).

It must be said that myths have long been interpreted or changed in various ways for the purposes of propaganda, but political machinations aside, we again see the struggle between two forces: the cosmic-spiritual (white) with the earthly-vital (red). Who wins is a question of attitude: the spiritual principle (white), to which homage is also paid in the myth of the Holy Grail, or the red principle of vital force, which Wales made its own.

Nidhogg

The dragon Nidhogg (*Níðhöggr* or Malice Striker, *nið* means envy) originates in Norse mythology. It is said to dwell among the roots of Yggdrasil, the World Tree, namely the very roots that lead to Niflheim, where it guards the spring of Hvergelmir (boiling spring). In the creation poem *Völuspá* from *The Poetic Edda*, Nidhogg is described as both a *nadr* (serpent) and a *dreki* (dragon), as we have already seen in other examples.

According to legend, Nidhogg lives off the dead who have lied or committed murder or adultery. When eating these dead people gives him digestive problems, Nidhogg gnaws on the roots of the World

Tree. This could threaten the stability of the entire world, so Urd, Verdandi, and Skuld, the three Norns, heal the wounds of the tree roots with a paste made from mud, so that balance is maintained.

Nidhogg also represents the antithesis of the eagle (a hawk in some myths) Vedrfölnir (the pale one), who lives in the branches of the World Tree. Ratatöskr, the red squirrel, carries (garbled) messages to and fro between the bird and the dragon.

Our knowledge of the mythological world view of the Germanic peoples is based on written sources produced between the 8th and the 13th centuries, including, among others, the poems *Grimnismál* and *Völuspá*, and Snorri Sturlson's *Prose Edda*. These sources date from the time when Christianity had already become widespread and there is no doubt that Christian ideas shaped and changed these written accounts. The moral element of the story describing Nidhogg eating the dead who have brought guilt upon themselves is certainly influenced by Christian dogma, but it is likely that older myths and legends were not subject to this same influence.

In Nidhogg we recognize a primordial power with strong chthonic (earth-related) features representing the antithesis of Vedrfölnir, the eagle (hawk), which is, on the other hand, spiritual and cosmic. Here, in the earthly realm, the souls of the ancestors are also received. Closely related with these is the fertility of the Earth, which is symbolically expressed in Hvergelmir (spring/well). Nidhogg, therefore, (originally) stood guard over the source of Earth's fertility and the world of the ancestors, the gateway to Niflheim. The dragon represents the primordial power of the Earth, within which rebirth, symbolized by the serpent shedding its skin, is also inherent. For many Indo-European peoples the ability to shed skin and undergo symbolic rebirth represented the death and regrowth of plants with the seasons, and also the death and rebirth of the human soul.

In many myths the serpent or the dragon are closely associated with the World Tree, the *axis mundi*, the axis of the world that links the cosmos and matter. The dragon Ladon on the tree of the Hesperides, and the serpent on the Tree of Knowledge and/or Life in Judeo-Christian tradition also reflect this association. And in many myths this dragon/serpent has a bird as its counterpart, generally an eagle: in India the naga's counterpart is the eagle Garuda.

Nidhogg is a therefore the prime example of a dragon as portrayed in cultures with a matrifocal world view that subsequently underwent a transformation in the patriarchal culture of the later Germanic peoples, and ultimately in Christianity—changing from a guardian of the life force and the ancestors to a devourer of sinners and a destroyer of the world order.

Apopis

In Egyptian mythology, the demon god Apopis (Apophis, Apep) embodied chaos, darkness, and dissolution. He was associated with natural phenomena such as storms and earthquakes, echoing the dragon as a symbol of primordial power. He is documented as far back as the Middle Kingdom and took the form of a giant serpent (sometimes also a turtle). Apopis was said to have lived in the sea of primordial chaos since the beginning of time, before creation.

The great enemy of the serpent/dragon Apopis is the sun god Ra, who by day crosses the sky in his solar ship and fills the world with light. When Ra sinks beneath the horizon, however, he travels through the underworld, where each night Apopis tries to devour both Ra and his ship. Every sunrise heralds another victory of Ra over the dragon, with the red of the rising and setting sun being proof of the bloody and bitter struggle between the two opponents. Solar eclipses reveal those brief moments when Apopis sought to consume Ra.

According to inscriptions in the Temple of Esna, Apopis was born from the saliva of the ancient goddess Neith (in Neith cosmology, Ra and Apopis are brothers). When the gods spurned him, Apopis swore revenge on Ra, the creator of the world. Other gods stand by Ra in his conflict with Apopis, however: Isis, Ra's companion, distracts the dragon, and Bastet beheads him, but Apopis is able to reassemble his body, and so the conflict between primordial chaos and creative power, between the conscious and unconscious, between day and night, begins eternally anew, a conflict that has many parallels with the struggle between Osiris and Seth.

Nessie

The legend of Nessie, the water dragon or so-called monster said to live in Loch Ness, the lake with the largest volume of fresh water in the Scottish Highlands, is already many hundreds of years old. In the year 565, a follower of the Irish monk and missionary Columba is said to have been swimming across the loch when a dragon surfaced "with a great roar and a wide-open mouth." People standing on the shore were paralyzed with fear, but St Columba hurried to the spot and made the sign of the cross, calling upon the Almighty and crying, "Go no further. Do not touch the man. Go back at once!" Nessie then disappeared beneath the surface of the water and is said to have lived peacefully in Loch Ness ever since, causing no harm, and sightings are still reported.

The dragon, affectionately nicknamed Nessie by locals, hit the head-lines again in the 1930s, when Dr. Robert Wilson published a photo-graph showing the silhouette of a long-necked creature reminiscent of a plesiosaur. For almost sixty years, the photo was considered by many to be authentic and proof of the monster's existence. In 1994, however, Dr. Wilson's son-in-law admitted that the monster was indeed a fake, photographed at long range.

The legend surrounding the dragon and the repeated eyewitness accounts have made Loch Ness the most famous lake in Scotland, with Nessie tourism being centered in the village of Drumnadrochit at the water's edge. Over the years many theories have been put forward to explain the sightings. Some believe Nessie to be the descendant of a dinosaur, others think it must be a giant sturgeon (enormous specimens of this fish do indeed live in the local rivers), and finally some disturbances seen on the surface of the lake have been attributed to whirlpools caused by tremors in the volcanic loch floor. The strike-slip fault zone of the Great Glen Fault, one of the largest in the country, runs through the loch and Italian geologist Luigi Piccardi has associated a much-reported strange "roaring" sound with seismic activity and the rumbling made by an earth tremor. In the original version of the legend of St Columba, the dragon appeared *cum ingenti fremitu* (with great tremors) and then disappeared back into the waters *tremefacta* (shuddering), a possible indication of the power of the Earth, manifested here in the loch.

The dragon as a symbol of the primordial powers of the Earth is an ancient mythological image. The Picts, an ancient people of northern Scotland, are said to have paid homage to this power at Loch Ness in the legend of the kelpie (a shape-shifting spirit that usually takes the form of a water horse). The loch is a place where the dragon power of the Earth is alive.

The Dragon in
Geomantic Symbolism

We have discussed the basic symbolic power of the dragon and the serpent, and have looked at some examples of well-known dragon figures. The dragon/serpent motif is closely linked with the idea of the *axis mundi*, the axis of the world. As already described, dragons and serpents were animals sacred to the Earth Mother, the Great Goddess. It was only with the advent of the patriarchy that they became the incarnation of evil, foes to be slain by male heroes: Heracles killed the dragon Ladon, Yahweh slew the primordial dragon Rahab, Thor conquered the Midgard Serpent, and so on.

Nomadic peoples followed the Earth dragon, on the trail of the "earthforces." In the places where they stopped and built sacred sites, dragon legends and place names such as Limburg or Wurmlingen exist to this day, referencing the dragon-like beast of the lindwyrm. If you were to look at the positions of such places on a map, you might be surprised to discover that they are located along a perfectly straight line. The Old High German word for dragon was *trahho* (track), another term for path or way. Clearly, the "dragon lines" denoted—at least spiritually—paths that ran in a straight line across the country (not to be confused with the specific geomantic phenomenon of a dragon line, see page 69). What is meant here is the alignment with the symbolism of dragon power. This may or may not correspond to a dragon line.

Many legends have also arisen around such paths along which spirits or the undead are said to follow a direct route between churches and graveyards; you can even find "paths for the dead" referred to on some maps. In Ireland it is said that the fairy folk follow straight lines of this kind. Known in geomancy as ley lines (see page 66), they could therefore be termed "paths of the spirit." Their relationship to the afterlife and the other world becomes clear upon closer examination. The ley line at Knowlton in England crosses three burial mounds and a ruined Norman church; another ley line in Cairo passes through eight mosques as well as the tombs of Al-Muzaffar, Yussef Bey, and Hassan Sadaqa. Each of these structures is in perfectly straight alignment and many places of worship along the ley line are dedicated to dragon slayers.

Rothenburg, Switzerland

Dragon symbolism is therefore closely linked with certain precisely designated places, some of which seem to be closer to dragon power than others. Objects that clearly exist in the real world are also often associated with mythical beings, one such being the dragon stone of Rothenburg in the Canton of Lucerne, in Switzerland, which can now be seen in Lucerne's Museum of Natural History. The following legend relates to this stone.

On a hot and oppressive day in 1420, Stempflin the farmer and his workers were heading out to the fields near Rothenburg to cut hay when they saw a dreadful dragon approaching them from Mount Rigi. It dipped and flew low over the farmers before heading off in the direction of Mount Pilatus. The heat and especially the foul smell emanating from the fabulous creature were so strong that the farmer blacked out. When he recovered, he noticed that the dragon had dropped something near him. Growing curious, he and his servants approached the "oozing slurry," which they understood to be spilt blood. Stempflin poked his stick into the porridge-like mass and it collapsed; within it, he found a dragon stone.

Fig. 13a. The dragon stone at Rothenburg, Lucerne,
in an historic print and the stone in the museum.

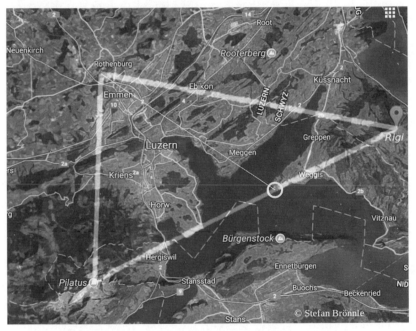

Fig. 13b. A geometric study of the landscape between
Rothenburg and the Pilatus and Rigi mountains.

The dragon stone was thought to have great healing powers. The
farmer Stempflin is said to have taken the stone (about the size of a
billiard ball) home and cleaned it. The markings on the outside of the
stone are reminiscent of waves or flames and it has been examined

57

many times. The historiographer Martin Schryber (1509–1531) named the material of the stone "draconite." At first it was assumed to be a meteorite, but investigations using modern CT scanning have shown that the stone is made entirely of clay. It does seem to have enhanced levels of radioactivity, however.

The trajectory of the dragon's flight as described in the legend would immediately suggest a geomantic line (dragon line/ley line) between the peaks of Rigi and Pilatus. Both mountains are rich in mythology and lie to the east and west of Lake Lucerne, with Mount Pilatus considered the epitome of a dragon mountain locally. Admittedly, Rothenburg is not located along this line and the places mentioned in the legend form a triangle. However, if you divide the distance between the peaks of Rigi and Pilatus into the golden ratio, the distance from this division point to Mount Pilatus equals the distance from Pilatus to Rothenburg. Does the dragon stone reflect a symbolic geometry within the landscape?

Basel, Switzerland

Another place linked with dragons is Basel. Various legends associate the city with a basilisk, a kind of dragon. When the city was founded, a basilisk was said to have lived in a cave by what is now the Gerberbrunnen fountain, and it is honored on the city's coat of arms. As the words basilisk and Basilea (an ancient name for the city) are similar to Basel, the inhabitants associated the two, but in reality the city name is not likely to have had anything to do with a basilisk originally. The first recorded mention of the town is in a Roman history, although another version of the story maintains that a merchant brought a basilisk to Basel. It is certainly true that a rooster was condemned to death in Basel in 1474 (following a fair trial, of course!); it had been accused of laying an egg, considered against the natural order of things. The people of Basel were especially afraid that a basilisk might emerge from the egg. After due process had been concluded, the rooster was beheaded and the offending egg consigned to the flames.

Basel Minster also has a fine "dragon stone," with the body outlined in black against the white stone and the head red, and set into the floor

Fig. 14. The dragon in the floor of Basel Minster.

a little to one side of the central aisle, an accumulation point for a "mountain" and "water" dragon (to use a feng shui term). In Basel the dragon is also directly associated with three women: three mountains located around the city, with the minster at the center, are dedicated to the female saints Margaret, Odile, and Chrischona.

A splendid symbolic representation of the spirit of place can also be seen on the capital of a column in Basel Minster: two creatures with the bodies of birds and the heads of dragons (presumably a reference to the legend of the Basel basilisk) enter the body of a figure through the ears, to be breathed out of the mouth and sink down into the bowels of the Earth before rising again to the genitals. The ear is considered an analogy for the whole human body, and in acupuncture is understood as a holon of the body. In a Christian context, the ear represents the spiritual body: *Gaude virgo, mater christi, quae per aurem concepisti* (Rejoice, O virgin, Mother of Christ, who conceived through the ear). Conception through the ear (*conceptio per aurem*) represents an immediate spiritual acceptance. The inspiration, literally the "breathing in," is immediately received in the entire soul. The same is true of the carving on the capital; the power of the place, symbolized by the two basilisk-like animals, flows directly into and inspires the human being.

Fig. 15. Capital in Basel Minster.

The human figure, now suffused with this *genius loci*, is then immediately spurred into action and breathes out the dragon figures again. Much like the divine breath of life into Adam, the human being becomes a creator being, and just as God once breathed life into the first human, a human breathes out again the spirit of the place that inspired them. These forces, transformed by human action, descend to the Earth, becoming physical and material. Human creative power is manifesting itself.

Finally, the two dragon heads rise back up from the Earth, entwine around the figure's legs to end, mouths open, in the figure's lap. The spirit of place in its entirety, its primal power transformed by a human being and turned into physical form, now itself exerts an effect on the figure. The womb, the sexual organs, are symbols of creativity, and *gens* (generation in the sense both of the generative organs and the human line of descent) is simultaneously influenced by the power of the place.

This simple and yet profound representation depicts the mutual fertilization of place and person. Basel Minster becomes a "power of place become form" that, in its turn, influences the people of the place.

It is a wonderful symbol for the interaction between human beings and the Earth.

Freising, Germany

Deep underground, in the crypt of Freising Cathedral, Germany, is the unique Bestiensäule (pillar of beasts), a carved stone column. The crypt contains eight rows of three pillars—twenty-four pillars in all. The number eight in number symbolism represents the connection of two worlds, so both baptismal and funerary chapels were eight-sided, reflecting the meeting of two worlds in these places. The number three represents the totality of a human being (body, spirit, and mind), and in the World Tree, three is evident in the Three Worlds (Lower, Middle, and Upper). Body, soul, and mind unite in this place, in this world and the next.

Fig. 16. The pillar of beasts in the crypt of Freising Cathedral.

Twenty-four pillars, twelve hours of day and twelve hours of night represent life and death, waking and sleep, the principle of light and darkness. In the center stands the pillar of beasts: on its west side, dragons rise up, while on the opposite side a woman with spiral braids sits with a plant in her hand. The rather banal Christian interpretation is that the dragons symbolize evil, the woman is the Virgin Mary, and the plant or flower is the delicate bloom of the church. In my opinion, the image is more archetypical, however. Here, where two worlds collide, where light and shadow meet, is the center of the world. Primordial power rises in the west—dragons are ancient symbols of the Earth's elemental power: the serpent sheds its skin and regenerates itself, carrying within it the primordial power of rebirth. The dragon elevates this power still further; in the west, it embodies the power of the earthly. Dragons can also be seen at the feet of the woman on the eastern side of the pillar, forming the basis of her strength and power. The woman is none other than the Great Goddess herself. Her braids are wound in a spiral, an ancient symbol of life as it twists and turns.

In her hand, the goddess holds the World Tree that stands in the center of the Earth, connecting the planes of reality. She guards, preserves, and protects the tree. At her feet, the motif of the World Tree is repeated very clearly and resembles the Irminsul (a palm-like tree) at the cult site of the Externsteine (rock formations) in the Teutoburg Forest in Germany.

The pillar of beasts depicts the foundation and core of our world, our very existence: the primordial power of the Earth (the dragon), the Great Goddess, the World Tree that links the planes of reality. This creates an abundance (eight rows of pillars) for body, soul, and mind (pillars in groups of three). Ancient, archaic wisdom from the earliest days of Christianity has been embodied and preserved in the heart of the cathedral building.

Munich, Germany

Two legends originating in Munich describe a "sacred line." One concerns the lindwyrm (see page 27) that is said to have taken up residence on the Marienplatz square, and the other involves the twelve

Fig. 17. The "wyrm corner" on Munich's Neues Rathaus (City Hall), where the lindwyrm is said to have emerged from the Earth.

apostles, who are said to process from the Church of the Holy Ghost to the Frauenkirche on Ember days (four days of penance in the Catholic church at the beginning of each quarter). If you were to draw a straight line between the two churches, you would find that the Wurmeck (wyrm corner), marked by a bronze dragon on the new City Hall, lies on the line. If the line were to be extended to the northwest, the churches of St Benno and St Boniface would also be on the line, while if extended to the southwest, the churches of St Wolfgang and Maria Ramersdorf (an 11th-century pilgrimage church) would be on the line. Here too, the dragon is associated with two pilgrimage churches (the Frauenkirche and Maria Ramersdorf) that are dedicated to the Virgin Mary.

We could add to these further dragon legends, such as those from the Drachenfels (Dragon's Rock) on the Rhine, the St Beatus Caves on Lake Thun in Switzerland, and many more. It is clear that dragon myths have very specific connections to the places with which they are associated. And in Chartres, in France, according to yet another legend, a *wouivre* (Earth serpent) lives in the ground below Chartres.

The symbol of the dragon is also linked with special geomantic phenomena, however, which are examined later (see page 69).

Dragon Paths

Dragon paths are part of the Earth's plane of primordial power. They consist predominantly of Earth ether (ether associated with the Earth element, based on the four elemental ethers) and are often connected with ancient pilgrimage paths. Side paths may leave the main dragon routes and spiral in on themselves; old churches or pre-Christian religious sites are often found at the center of the spirals.

The term "dragon path" was coined by geomantic practitioner Johanna Markl, while Marko Pogačnik describes dragon paths as follows in his book *Das geheime Leben der Erde* (The secret life of the Earth).

> *The nourishing system associated with the plane of atomic energy does not belong to the life processes of the Earth's surface. If it is applied on the plane of manifested life, it brings about death and destruction. However, the European geomantic tradition knows of a secret path on which these dragon powers may touch the manifested plane of life. It points to the so-called "dragon paths," paths on which dragons move through the landscape in secret. They leave a trail of life-giving powers that can be received by living creatures, including humans, in the particular surroundings.*
>
> *Translated into rational language, this mythical image implies that the immediate presence of nuclear forces, the basis of the life force, would have a destructive effect if encountered directly; but these forces become*

accessible when they leave an ethereal impression "on the reverse of the Earth's surface." This impression can be perceived as an organic stream of fiery energy; it stays close to the ground and floats along with a slow and majestic rhythm.

We can also think of dragon paths as streams of the sexual force of the Nature goddess, which fertilizes every aspect of its kingdom.

In pre-Christian times, pilgrimage paths were often laid along these lines to celebrate the Earth's sexual forces and Gaia's life-giving powers. This tradition was still followed in the Middle Ages, when many churches were frequently sited along such "dragon paths" to ensure a proper balance between the sexual powers of the Earth and the spiritual powers of the universe.

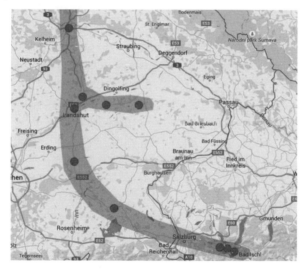

Fig. 18. Dragon path showing churches dedicated to
St Wolfgang in South Germany.

St Wolfgang is also closely linked with prehistoric cup stones and springs at religious sites. This perpetually roaming historical monk is therefore regarded as the founder of countless churches that are associated with spring and stone cults. As these sites are often situated adjacent to one another like pearls on a string, there is plenty of evidence for a theory of ancient pilgrimage routes that predate Christianity. In particular, from Regensburg via Landshut (with an offshoot to the east) and continuing south before heading east in the Chiemgau area in Bavaria, a well-documented path passes the churches of St Wolfgang associated with spring and stone worship sites. It leads via St Gilgen beside Lake Wolfgang on the north side of the lake over the Falkenstein castle to reach St Wolfgang im Salzkammergut, also on Lake Wolfgang: from a geomantic perspective, this is a dragon path.

Ley Lines

The concept

In the 1920s British businessman, self-taught archeologist, and author Alfred Watkins discovered that prehistoric religious sites in the British Isles such as stone circles, menhirs, and hilltop forts, as well as the intersections of ancient streets and Christian churches, were often found to be located along perfectly straight lines in what he termed an "alignment." The churches were frequently located in places bearing the suffix "-ley" (such as Hinckley, Camberley, or Crawley), so he named these alignments "leys." In Old English the word means something like "clearing" or "fallow land," and so corresponds to place names in Germany that end in "-rode" or "-rade," indicating cleared land.

To understand the significance of the term "ley line," we should first ask ourselves how places are named in general. It is obvious that names often derive from distinguishing features, something that makes one place different from another, such as "crooked peak" or "blue lake," and so on. At the time when such places were named, bare areas of land devoid of vegetation would have been something of an exception, suggesting that these places would have tended to be early settlements. In Old Saxon, *leia* often means a "rock" (cf. the Loreley outcrop of rock on the River Rhine). Rocks are normally by their very nature open and clear of vegetation.

One theory suggests that the places with the suffix "-ley" were naturally deforested areas linked by routes that were easier to walk along than others and which in time became accepted ancient paths. The word ley (or lea, meaning "meadow") may have been used colloquially to denote a path (in the sense of a path across a field). So what kind of places are free of vegetation? Places that are too wet or too rocky for plants to grow—and such locations would, in turn, have been unsuitable for settling, since only fertile land was suitable for agriculture. This could support the theory that the line of arrangement itself, the alignment, stunts growth without having a detrimental or indeed beneficial effect on the surroundings. However, water diviners tracing the leys described by Alfred Watkins reported a noticeable twitching of divining rods. Energetic ley lines had been discovered.

The phenomenon

Ley line is one of the most common concepts in geomancy. In the first instance it simply describes an alignment, a number of significant places strung out along a straight line. However, as mentioned, water

Fig. 19. Analysis of a ley line.

diviners have noticed rod (or pendulum) reactions along such lines. The structure of the various water divining reaction zones often differ so dramatically from each other that a variety of structurally different phenomena must be assumed. Terms associated with or relevant to ley lines include dragon line, energy line, Earth meridian, Margaret line, and geomantic zone, among others. Therefore the ancient concept of a ley is distinct from the energetic phenomenon to which the term now refers.

The dragon

Since churches standing on ley lines and forming an alignment often have dragon slayers as patron saints (St George, St Michael, St Beatus, St Margaret, and so on), ley lines are closely associated with dragon symbolism. A ley could even be described as a recumbent dragon! The life-giving, elemental power of the Earth is given formal expression in this geomantic phenomenon. The energy of the ley line extending in a straight line over several miles (or sometimes many hundreds of miles) is essentially ethereal, but if plotted on a map, it can certainly meander a little from the straight. The core area of a ley line is tubular, although strong eddies in the ether can also occur beyond it. Spiritual information, which may feature as recurring symbols or motifs in churches standing on ley lines, is often also carried in the ethereal field of this core area. The best known of these is probably the "Grail line" described by Jens M. Möller, German author and pioneer of geomancy, which crosses Europe from east to west. Places are located along it that, in one way or another, are associated with the myth of the Holy Grail—such as the church in the small village of Wolframs-Eschenbach, hometown of the famous German medieval author Wolfram von Eschenbach, whose epic poem *Parzival* describes the hero's quest for the Grail.

As far as sacred architecture is concerned, ley lines represent large-scale phenomena that link various religious sites both energetically and on a mental/spiritual level, much like different acupuncture points on a meridian. Comparison can be made with kundalini (the spiritual energy located at the base of the spine), energetic power that

when awakened can move up through the body to expand aware-
ness and consciousness. Ley lines could be described as the kundalini
channels of planet Earth.

Dragon Lines

The term "dragon lines" is a prime example of just how varied the terminology in geomancy can be. Ley line can be used as a blanket term
to describe very different phenomena, and yet the same phenomena
can be described individually using various other terminology too, as
the concept of dragon lines so clearly illustrates.

Author Marko Pogačnik has been using the term dragon line since
around 1997, having previously referred to the phenomenon as "spiritual ley lines." On the other hand, geomantic practitioner Hans-Jörg
Müller has been referring to the Margaret line since the early 1990s,
after discovering it during the course of (joint) research in a church
dedicated to St Margaret (a slayer of dragons). Dragon line, on the other
hand, derives from the terminology used by geomantic practitioner
Johanna Markl.

What is a dragon line?
Like ley lines, when plotted on a map, dragon lines also extend in a
straight line for many miles (in the classical sense, they are by definition
also ley lines). Unlike a ley line (described by Marko Pogačnik as a
"power ley"), however, a dragon line is far more spiritual, with only
a few ethereal structures present.

Places located on dragon lines have been used for religious purposes
for centuries. Megalithic relics (menhirs, dolmens) and legends with
strong matrifocal associations (veneration of the Great Goddess) are
not uncommon. It is also notable that churches located along these lines
are frequently (but not always, of course) dedicated to female saints.

Dragon lines are very firmly located in the sphere of the Earth's
elemental power (the planet's primordial spiritual space). We are
accustomed to seeing the physical Earth and the spiritual cosmos as

opposites, but the Earth too possesses a spiritual space within it. If we compare ley lines with the kundalini channel, dragon lines would represent spiritual connections, associations that are linked with one another in a spiritual space.

Although both geomantic phenomena are very closely aligned, a ley line is more aptly described as the power aspect (or red aspect), while a dragon line describes the spiritual aspect (or white aspect). My research has shown that the two aspects commonly coincide at sanctuaries dedicated to female goddesses in pre-Christian times, or churches dedicated to the Virgin Mary in particular, where a dragon and a ley line often meet and cross. The temple complexes of Ħaġar Qim and Mnajdra on Malta are at the junction of a ley line and a dragon line. There is an interplay of vital energy and the physical (ley line) together with the Earth-related and the spiritual (dragon line). In churches such as the pilgrimage church of St Mary's in the Thalkirchen area of Munich, Germany, or indeed in the city's Frauenkirche (which is also a Marian pilgrimage site), the power aspect and spiritual aspect of the Earth also meet in the form of a ley line and a dragon line.

Dragon lines offer people an opportunity for direct access to the Earth's elemental spiritual space, the Earth cosmos, and indeed to the consciousness of the Earth.

Dragon lines: the inner perspective

Like ley lines, dragon lines map out a network on the Earth. While power ley lines tend to be (but not exclusively) present in their vital-energetic effects, dragon lines are located on the spiritual, elemental level of the Earth.

In one of my geomantic training seminars (Gaia's Body: The Way of Earthkeepers), I led a trance journey to dragon lines (taking inspiration from American linguist and anthropologist Felicitas Goodman). Adopting a special, trance-inducing posture and accompanied by the beat of a drum, the participants connected with the dragon lines in order to experience them from within, as it were. See opposite for a summary of their experiences.

Dragons and snakes

Dragons and snakes were frequently perceived, with the participants' experiences ranging from seeing a powerful dragon's eye and a crowned serpent slithering through water, to taking a ride on a dragon or even flying through the air as a dragon oneself. This is where the mythological image of the dragon (serpent) emerges, which also gives its name to these primordial power lines on the Earth. The dragon is deeply anchored in the collective unconscious as a bearer of culture and consciousness.

Colors

The majority of the colors perceived were on a spectrum ranging from white to blue. One participant, for example, saw a line of women dressed in white moving along a white line, while another saw a white, fiery cord, with blue and white swirls. Bluish threads formed a net, next to which were seen swirls of fire, glowing coals, and lava. I myself perceived the dragon line as a tunnel of light and sensed it as "soul fire." The light pulsed outward.

A network

The dragon lines perceived during the trance journeys clearly took on the appearance of a network. In one case, this was simply a network of energy lines, sometimes with others branching off them, or they took the form of channels of dark water. I myself initially saw a figure (Gaia) wrapped in fine fabric with an irregular woven pattern. This fabric descended over the landscape and the Earth lit up where the individual threads touched the ground.

A network of books—a kind of world library—formed another image. One female participant saw galaxies in space that were interconnected. This "star consciousness," the information from this cosmic network, flowed into the network of the Earth. We experience dragon lines as a system of profound, inner cosmic knowledge through which the Earth is connected to the cosmos.

Wounds

Significant damage to the network caused by humans was also seen. In my own case, the fabric in which Gaia was wrapped was riddled with scorched burn holes. Others also saw rips in the fabric through which energy was draining away and tried to repair them during the trance journey. Areas that were inaccessible were also seen, like areas grayed out on a computer screen. This shows the effects of humanity as a whole, which has largely disconnected itself from Nature and the consciousness of the Earth, disrupting Gaia's spiritual/energetic fabric.

What was indeed astonishing was the great synergy of the images and experiences that a purely radiesthetic recording (work with a pendulum or dowsing rod reflects the body's subtle unconscious reactions to energy fields) of the geomantic lines would never have revealed.

Soul Paths

A long, long time ago, a man was working in his cellar at midnight when, from one corner of the room, a large serpent came sliding toward him. In its open mouth was a key. Its red tongue flicked back and forth and it approached with shrill hisses. Although the man's knees were trembling, he overcame his fear and tore the key from its mouth. All at once, the cellar was filled with a great light and he saw a door. Opening it, he found a long passageway(!), and the more he advanced along it, the brighter the walls seemed to shine and the stronger the light with every step; it seemed as if he were surrounded by an enormous bed of glowing coals. At the end of the passageway, there was a great hall full of treasure and a poor soul waiting to be released. After a few steps, however, the man's courage failed and he fell backward, head over heels. When he reached the door to the cellar once more, there was a dull thud, the door shut, and he was left standing in complete darkness. He could not get the vision of the great treasure out of his head, however, and the next day, he went back down into the cellar in the hope

that at midnight, the door would open again. The next morning,
he was found dead beside the cellar door.

This myth from the Waldviertel region of Austria contains elements of a near-death experience, such as the luminous tunnel, but also the motif of the serpent carrying a key. The entrance is underground, a symbolic reference to the fact that the path leads to the otherworldly realm of the afterlife, the hall full of treasure. This myth is one of a series of legends about the world beyond, such as the folklore motif of the wild hunt, also from Austria's Waldviertel. If the places in these legends were to be marked on a map and a line drawn between them, it would reveal a meandering route, a so-called soul path.

Soul paths connect various otherworldly spaces close to the Earth sphere (ancestral places) and are touched at certain intervals by radiation and angelic focal points. A non-incarnate consciousness can, of course, choose whichever path it likes, but soul paths are "illuminated" by spiritual forces. Imagine you are alone in the forest at night. You can go wherever you like, but a distinct, marked path that is brightly lit by moonlight is a more attractive proposition than wandering haphazardly through the dark woods. It is much the same with soul paths; they are illuminated by the consciousness of the Earth (in other words, the serpent) and by the impulses of angelic focal points, which is why "excarnate" beings (souls without a body), far prefer to take these paths rather than others.

Similarly, some near-death experiences also report the sensation of being moved in a horizontal plane. The American hypnotherapist Dr. Michael Newton recounts an extract from a session with a near-death experience:

Dr. Newton: Can you describe in more detail how your soul travels along these lines of contact?
K: It is simply more targeted, as if my soul were being guided along a line to a destination. It is as if I were in a current of white water, but not as dense as water because the current is lighter than air.

This experience chimes closely with my own. Soul paths consist of soul water, so to speak (see below). The path to the other world is closely interwoven with the Earth serpent as a symbol. As already mentioned, just as the snake sheds its skin, the soul also discards its shell. Soul paths are therefore often associated with the symbol of the serpent (less commonly, the dragon) in churches. In geomantic terms, they represent a certain astral aspect of the elemental force discussed in this book; as formal phenomena, they correspond in a certain way to the star serpent (or celestial serpent) on which the *ba* (a part of the soul) of the pharaoh rides into the astral sphere of the stars. Seen from this perspective, soul paths are the otherworldly aspect of the serpent or dragon symbol.

Soul Water

Soul water is another phenomenon that is indirectly associated with dragon power, even if it is not obvious from the term itself. This may be a new concept to some readers, but it often crops up in spiritual literature and in myths in one form or another.

And the earth was without form, and void; and darkness was upon the face of the deep. And the spirit of God moved upon the face of the waters (Genesis 1:2). Since, in this passage from the Christian Bible, light has yet to be created, the text is clearly not describing a physical evolutionary phase. "Darkness was upon the face of the deep"— the light of consciousness has not yet reached the Earth, only the divine spirit is present, and yet water is clearly in existence. This is not physical water, however, but an earlier form that precedes the physical substance. Soul water describes a spiritual fluid, which in Hebrew is known as מִיַם, *majim*, powerful primordial water.

In the myth recorded in the Finnish epic saga *Kalevala*, Luonnotar swims in the endless ocean and sings Earth and sky into existence with her creation song. Creation and soul water are closely connected. In the Hindu creation myth, the primordial ocean क्षीराब्धि *Kṣīrābdhi* is a sea of milk that takes on solid form through churning.

Soul water represents a preliminary form of materiality that is "animated," or rather "inspired." Founder of anthroposophy Rudolf Steiner calls it "water-earth." *This water-earth is at the same time the origin, the primordial source of all substance found on Earth, all external substance, whether contained in minerals, plants, animals, or human beings. This substance that every terrestrial being carries within itself is present in this water-earth, volatilized into the astral plane.* (GA 96, p.34 of the Rudolf Steiner Archive).

A little earlier, Steiner writes that this water-earth from which the Earth was once made exists to this day in the so-called fourth layer of the Earth; *in this layer, substances are such that they are imperceptible to any external sense, they are in an astral state.* Steiner uses the word astral in two contexts. In one sense it is derived from *astra,* the Latin word for star, so astral is related to stellar forces. In the second, related context, astral also means spiritual, the soul, and in this sense, Steiner's water-earth is not only a meta-form of the physical but also spiritual in its very essence, which explains the use of the term.

Soul water is a very fine, astral, fluid-like presence in the depths of the Earth's strata. As a pre-material condition of the Earth, it is closely related with the power of the Creator, and matter evolved from it. According to Rudolf Steiner, this process was completed when the Moon separated from the Earth, which is why the Moon controls the oceans on Earth to this day; *when the Moon was expelled, the transformation was complete.* (GA 106, p.89f)

As an astral layer in the depths of the Earth, soul water is also closely associated with dragon power, hence the need to mention it here. Dragons are associated with water in countless myths; in East Asia they bring rain and guarantee the fertility of the fields, and ancient dragons often take the form of sea monsters.

Dragon power is the vehicle of life on Earth, permeating sexuality, creativity, the vitality of plants, and the breath of animals and humans. Dragon power is the life force that forms the basis for Gaia's activity. Rudolf Steiner refers to this too when he describes early (but not yet physical) human beings as half dragon, half light-being. Here, humans appear as the soul connection between the cosmos and Gaia: *In that time, humans were floating, swimming in the mass of the Earth. . .* (GA 106, p.89f) This state of floating in astral water—soul water—just like Luonnotar in the Finnish creation myth, is also the paradisal, heavenly state, as it were. The paradisal world sphere of the Earth essentially consists of soul water (Marko Pogačnik also calls it the Earth cosmos). The soul water of the Earth is astral, dependent on the power of the stars.

In the soul water of the Earth, we therefore have a special Earth layer that in a geomantic sense is of enormous importance for evolution, for the current life force on Earth, for the path after death and, of course, for the development of the Earth itself. It is closely intertwined with both stellar forces and the dragon power of the Earth.

It is precisely this soul water that plays an important role in the current process of the Earth's transformations, the time of change. At present, ever greater amounts are being released from the depths of the Earth and so are increasingly available to Earth's creatures. As geomancer and shaman Sibylle Moana Krähenbühl explained in her trance account:

Gaia will manifest herself anew. Gaia will change some things. Working from her own cosmic being, she has begun to use the all-connecting fine structures of the white fabric of the soul of this world to deeply embed the consciousness of the stars in the water worlds of the Earth's spheres. She is renewing the power of the stars in the elemental planes.

Gaia is currently working powerfully in water and in soul water, cleansing and extending it. Our heart space is very deeply connected with Gaia's soul water. She speaks about this soul water. She is the goddess of the landscape, and through this soul water weaves her consciousness into the land.

So the Earth interacts directly both with the material, traditional state of living creatures and also with cosmic powers, the astral forces, via soul water; it paves new paths for the journey after death and renews dragon power.

We can see quite clearly how dragons and serpents are far more than mere metaphors. In geomancy, they have a very real and perceptible aspect that can be experienced in certain places as a "local force," as well as being represented in various geomantic phenomena. We can therefore understand the dragon (as is also the case in Asian mythology) as a power that is changeable in form and all-pervading but that assumes a form in specific ethereal phenomena. In addition to the power aspect of the dragon is its consciousness, a consciousness that is most intimately fused with the Earth as a macro-being, endowing matter with an inner spirit.

If we term this power of consciousness and the life force of the Earth "dragon," a figure from fairy tales becomes an entity that can be experienced in real life, and its myths become ways of describing or portraying this power.

It is at this point that I would like to leave dragons as a pure metaphor, since I believe we find ourselves at a threshold. We have reached a "time of change," as both Sibylle Moana Krähenbühl and I put it, a time in which this dragon power is becoming increasingly discernible for many people.

A Time of Change
and a Time of Dragons:
When the Dragons Rise

I hope I have succeeded in describing the symbolism of serpents and dragons in all their diversity in myth and legend. As with descriptions of geomantic phenomena, I am increasingly keen to put to one side the dragon as a purely symbolic entity and focus instead on the essence and direct experience of serpents and dragons. In order to do so, I must change my writing style, especially when describing my deeply personal experiences. A comparative, abstract style is not suitable for describing experiences that have profoundly touched the very core of my being. I am hoping that the foundation laid in the previous chapters is sufficiently solid that readers will still be able to follow me in the subsequent pages. The metaphor has become a symbol, and the symbol will become a living creature.

The Shadow of the Dragon

We live in a world that no longer perceives the essential, the real, in the sense that something produces an effect, since this is not the materiality upon which our culture has learned to fixate so very firmly. The effect-producing (reality-forming) force is perceived only through the shadow that it casts in the physical world, much as we see in Plato's famous cave allegory.

This shadow can be distinct in different ways. It can be the observed wave-particle duality that in quantum mechanics describes two, in fact contradictory physical observations concealing the reality behind them. It can be a universe that appears to be expanding but contracting elsewhere at the same time, hinting at the reality lying beneath it. It can be the configuration of the universe itself, which is, by turns, assumed to be a sphere, Euclidian, or hyperbolic.

We must not lose ourselves in the infinite minutiae of the macro- or microcosmos, however. We have no doubt all experienced the effects of the nonmaterial at some point, perhaps in the momentary shifting of emotions, a change in mood, the perception of an "atmosphere" in a room, or other experiences that could not be entirely understood on a physical level.

We cannot grasp these materially because they are rooted in the immaterial world. We can describe life in biological terms by means of certain mechanisms, but we are unable to fully explain or understand it, since life, or vitality, lies in an immaterial reality, as paradoxical as this may sound, a "substance" (literally meaning "standing beneath")

Fig. 20. A dragon in shadow form.

of matter. Try as biology might to come up with chemical compounds, life simply does not emerge from them! And by the same token, if I may be permitted this sideswipe (!), we will never really understand health or being healthy by studying pathogens, and we will certainly not be able to bring about health by attempting to eliminate them. Life, and indeed health, are considerably more than biological describable functions such as respiration and metabolism, and more than the well-known five properties that define life (the use of energy, growth and development, metabolism, response to the environment, reproduction and cellular organization). By immersing ourselves in the "shadow," we turn away from the very reality that casts this shadow.

Those who suspect the shadow to be an imprint or replica and infer a higher reality (a non-ordinary reality) are laughed at and mocked by others all the more, and even on occasion challenged and fought.

In geomancy, the primordial life force principle that permeates the universe is known as the dragon. Laozi wrote in the classic Chinese philosophical text *Tao Te Ching* that a concept through which understanding is reached cannot address the inconceivable. His aim was to write about something numinous and yet fundamental that in essence could not be grasped. In order to do so, he needed a concept, however, and he chose *dao* (*tao*), which means "the path," but it is clear that this was no physical path. The very concept through which one can comprehend is not a path, although the term might suggest otherwise. In this sense, even the dragon inherent in matter is not a dragon, at least not in the sense of a monster that must be slain. Instead, this symbol stands for the consciousness of primordial power itself, and yet our human consciousness is designed in such a way that, when in contact with precisely this primordial power, it often creates images of dragons in order to "have an image through which we can imagine."

The dragon is both a symbol and an intrinsic consciousness, a metaphor and yet substantive reality. If we make use of the image (and the term) in geomantic phenomena (such as dragon lines, dragon paths, dragon veins—known as Longmei in China—dragon nests, mountain and water dragons, among others), it is because these are so close to the Earth's plane of elemental power, indeed to life itself in its most intrinsic form, although they are ultimately only shadows of the dragon. In these terms, finding the dragon within also means finding the power within us that, on a higher level of reality, is at the same time causal for both us and our life on Earth. Negating this level of reality, indeed fighting it, corresponds to the nature of our culture, which is at odds in countless battles with dragons with the elemental power of the Earth, indeed of the cosmos. The battle is therefore a battle of consciousness, with one side striving to focus upon the shadow and the other to look the dragon itself in the face. Absurdly, the latter is seen by adherents of the former as illusionary and fictitious, pure fantasy, in other words. Indeed, as long as emotions are regarded as imagination, as long as non-rational perception is treated with contempt, dragons will remain only a fantasy, and even the shadow only the effect cast by a passing cloud.

In this respect, so much more than a political conflict is taking place, particularly in this transitional period. It is the collective intuition that reality does not comprise a single truth, that it is multilayered, and that eliminating entire layers of reality can result in the death of the entire ecosystem as well as social and family structures. The dragon cannot be extracted from matter as a fantastical construct without then leaving the soulless shell of itself behind. Liberation of the dragon begins with recognizing its shadow, but it does not end there—indeed, far from it. It will transform the paradigms of thought.

Free Dragons

Our ancient relationship with the Earth is reflected in the fighting and slaying of dragons: what cannot be harnessed and made useful is destroyed. Exploitation or death, humanity seems to have left Earth's forces barely any other option. Just how different this makes the votive offering in the Heiligkreuz (Holy Cross) pilgrimage church in Entlebuch in Switzerland seem!

St Margaret (clad in black, white, and red) cradles the dragon in her arms like a precious infant in need of protection or like a beloved

Fig. 21. Votive image of St Margaret in the
Heiligkreuz church, Switzerland.

pet. There is no battle, no conflict. Female power and dragon power
are united in love.

It is time to free ourselves from the hostile approach of a St George
and instead embrace the loving devotion of a St Margaret. The dragon
powers that once roamed freely across the land should not be viewed
simply from a functional and profitable perspective. Far too often it is
a question of the benefit that something can bring us or what use can
be made of a place. We should instead ask ourselves what benefits we
can bring to the Earth.

It is time to let go of our need for control and to surrender ourselves
without fear to the Earth, to Nature, to life! A life of absolute control
is no life at all and does not even offer any pretense at security. Life,
real life, is always a risky business. We can be hurt by it (who hasn't
been hurt?), but if we remain entirely unscathed by life, we are merely
exhibits in a virtual museum.

Living dragon power means breathing freely, moving freely, living on
the Earth and encountering plants, animals, and people. We experience
the dragon power of life itself, the unbridled impulses and feelings that
flow through us when we are in love, when we take pleasure in something, when we allow our defenses to drop.

Free dragon power can be unsettling or even frightening because it is an unknown quantity for many. It is something strange and alien and yet so intimately connected with our life on Earth. That is why it is also time to face this unknown instead of fighting it with all our strength.

However intimate the relationship between Margaret and the dragon in the image may seem, the time to set the dragon free will eventually come. The young dragon will grow and mature, and eventually it will want to slip the leash. This instinct for free movement is a law of life itself. We recognize it in animals, plants, indeed even in the flow of water that cannot be kept dammed in reservoirs and canals forever. If we fail to allow unrestricted movement, life will sooner or later break free on its own—the plant will outgrow its trellis support, the animal will escape its cage, and the water will break its banks.

Let us get to know the dragon power within us, give it space, set it free. Only then will human beings (once again) understand what life really is!

A Time of Change: A Time of Chaos

In homeopathy, succussion (intense shaking) is one of the important processes in ensuring the "potentization" of a remedy, increasing its effectiveness. The founder of homeopathy Samuel Hahnemann described the process in a variety of ways, from "strong and sustained stirring" to "intimately mixed," "consistent and intimate mixing," "properly unified through diligent shaking," and "intimately unified through minutes of shaking." In "dynamization of the solution" via dilution, Hahnemann sees a way for the "spirit-like medicinal power" to separate from the medicinal molecules to be transferred to the carrier medium in potentized form. Nowadays, we would call this "information" but there's no disputing the fact that the process is ultimately a ritual one.

The process found to be the breakthrough in making the treatment more effective, therefore, is prior chaoticization. The moment of chaos would appear to be a state, or rather a dynamic, that at first sight seems opaque and unfathomable, a moment of "unbearable confusion."

The word chaos (from ancient Greek χάος *cháos*) does indeed originate in Greek mythology, meaning opposed to or at odds with the cosmos, the world order. Chaos is related to the Greek verb χαίνω *chainō* (yawn, gape), so chaos could be translated as a yawning void. In mythological terms, then, the chaos of the Greeks would be comparable with the yawning primordial void of Ginnungagap from Nordic myth. According to the Greek poet Hesiod (c. 700 BCE), Gaia is a descendant, a daughter of chaos, coming into being at the same time as her siblings Nyx (the darkness of the night), Erebos (the darkness of the underworld), Tartarus (the underworld) and Eros (love). With Gaia, the elemental forces of existence emerge from chaos.

The *tohu vavohu* (primordial chaos) of the Hebrew texts is similar. *Tohu* and (*va*) *vohu* correspond to the primeval Babylonian dragons Tiamat and Abzu. The mothers of the Earth (Gaia) are ultimately also the dragon powers that we perceive as chaotic and opposed to the order of the cosmos. In mythology, creation is born from chaos, life from apparent nothingness; it is permeated with dragon power and is the basis of Gaia.

In academic research, the concept of chaos is viewed differently from the way it is viewed and used colloquially. Chaos research is a subfield of nonlinear dynamics. It deals with order within dynamic systems whose development seems unpredictable. The equations on which it is based are deterministic, however; chaos research essentially identifies the order in chaos.

The Austrian naturalist and philosopher Viktor Schauberger also understood the formation of vortices in water as an ordered structure. Short-lived disturbances to water that result in a chaotic state are immediately equalized and balanced, leading directly to ordered spiral or helical ripples and movements that may nevertheless seem disordered to the observer. The water moves and flows through the vortex in apparent chaos into a higher energetic state.

Here we recognize chaos as a prime mover of elemental forces, creating a new order and higher states of being. Nevertheless, the moment of disturbance remains delicate, as it allows the "spirit-like medicinal power," present only in traces, to transfer itself to the entire carrier medium. This means that, in this state, the medium is open to all kinds of spiritual forces. Ultimately, it is the state of mind of the potentizer (person carrying out the potentization) that determines whether it is healing medicinal power or poison that penetrates the carrier medium with its information.

Socially, with the so-called and much-discussed Covid-19 pandemic, we are in a time of chaos. Many old systems have broken down, and the attacks on the Reichstag in Germany and the US Capitol (whether staged or not) are symbols of collapse and apparent chaos. The laws set out in government regulations (which are actually supposed to ensure things are "regular" in society) are resulting (not least through their illogicality) in ever greater confusion, in chaotic states that we need not list in greater detail here.

The carrier medium of society is in a state of whirlwind upheaval, and it is unlikely that the balance of power between parties and factions will be the same next year as it is today. The economy is also undergoing fast-paced change. Spiritually and socially, we find ourselves in the process of dilution and potentization. This makes the ritual aspect, spiritual power, now all the more important. What will determine the order that will no doubt reestablish itself? What spiritual forces will have spread among the carrier mass of society? The question is far more fundamental than the political left or right, mainstream or alternative, even "technocratic dictatorship" or "geocultural democracy." The moment of chaos that we are currently experiencing is releasing powerful emotions, which is a good thing in one respect, since they provide the energy for the quantum leap, but when emotions exhaust themselves in rage, hatred, and violence, they provide the stimulus for the core of the future new order. Whatever each individual's attitude to governmental measures may be (whether seen as necessary or negligently excessive), the ritual impulse of their basic spiritual attitude is far more fundamental. Each person, each faction must take the fears of the other seriously; this is not a question of intellectual discussion, but rather of emotional attention. No panic reaction must be allowed to cause us to poison this delicate moment of chaotic upheaval with hatred and violence. If we manage to keep our hearts open in this time of turbulence, the dragons will give birth to a new world out of the chaos, a renewal of Gaia! In this respect, we are experiencing dragon power in real life as those who are giving birth to a new order from chaos. This transitional time that has shaken our values, daily routines, and our ideas to the core is, as it were, the birth of the dragons. Much is being freed, much is being revealed.

I led several initiation cycles during the pandemic, and the opening of so-called dragon portals (see page 91) was perceived by many of the initiates as the harbingers, the forerunners of a new age. The first lockdown brought about a rapprochement between Nature and people; birds were singing as they had not done for years as they greeted the spring of 2020, dolphins took over harbors, and wild animals wandered down the streets of our cities. Elemental forces broke through once more. The terrible flood in Ahrweiler, Germany, should also be viewed in this context, when the power of the river obliterated its previous course. As we have established, freed dragons are clearly not cute and cuddly, but the moment of chaos opens up new portals of thought in us, new ways of thinking. We find ourselves in the midst of a "succussion" to shape the future for a new potential.

When Gaia Awakens

It was in the spring of 2018 that I was first inspired and tasked to initiate people into the power and connection with Gaia. A group of some fifteen people were accordingly connected with helper beings from the animal, vegetable, and mineral kingdoms, and from the plane of human ancestors. They received the key to opening up Gaia's field of consciousness and soul.

Several months then passed until I again felt the impulse to begin opening the portals to Gaia. The group became active. The portals were pulsating like a beating heart, emitting waves of multicolored light, and began to form a network, reaching far beyond the extent of the group's activities, into and around the world.

My perception of Gaia's awakening is of an animated life force rising up from the depths of the Earth and combining with the ethereal fabric of the land. At the same time, spirits that are powerfully linked with Gaia's consciousness are emerging from deep within the Earth and begin to work within the natural world. These involve ancient processes that began thousands of years ago and alienated humanity from the Earth. However, a kind of reconquest is slowly taking place. Something is changing in the soul of human beings, but it will not happen overnight—it may even take several generations—but it is beginning.

On the one hand, Nature's elemental beings seem to be abandoning and withdrawing completely from certain places in parallel with the exodus of insects, birds, and vertebrates. However, other beings remain as if biding their time expectantly and waiting for a specific change in the fabric of the human soul. It is not a question of the end of the world approaching or, by the same token, peace and happiness emerging to reign supreme in the world. It is more about reconciling humanity with the Earth once more, allowing spirits to do their work. As a result, humanity's decision-making, and ultimately its actions, will undergo change.

This gradual process begins where humanity once thought of itself as separate from the natural world and disregarded Earth in its eagerness to exploit Gaia's soul sphere for itself. Gaia is now awakening as if from a long dream, but this will not take place without significant crisis on the material plane. For too long human beings have derived sustenance and therefore life force from technology and artificial (chemical) fertilizers added to the soil. For too long they have woven a web of cold reason about the Earth, but this artificially produced sustenance, this life force, has been exhausted. Increases in food production will eventually tail off as the soil is exploited and becomes more and more exhausted, and these systems will collapse. In future it is only by cooperating with the forces of the Earth that human beings will be able to continue living in this wonderful world.

More and more people will start to feel the need to rethink and change their lives, their lifestyle, diet, behavior as consumers, and their respect for life as a whole. But those who derive profit from the status quo and denigrate the choices of others will fight against and challenge this, while ever greater distractions for the mind and soul seek to divert our attention.

In this awakening of Gaia, people will feel more vital and alive, more in touch with their souls, so that old ways of thinking and behaving can be broken and changed. We can nourish this force within ourselves by getting in touch with Nature.

- Lie down on the ground and breathe in the Earth's animated life force.
- Enjoy the physical touch of plants, trees, flowers, leaves, grass . . . with an open heart.
- Give animals their space, play an active role in protecting their habitats, and enjoy watching wild animals return (where this does take place) without fear.
- Leave some space in your garden for the rewilding of plants and wildlife.
- Replace "dead" areas of concrete, paving, and artificial grass with the living power of the plant kingdom.
- Give Nature due respect in your consumer behavior. Ask yourself what you really need.
- Sit down in the silence of Nature and imagine your consciousness expanding. It is slowly extending, pervading every tree, plant, beetle, and ant. Allow this to happen.
- Connect with the essence of the Earth's soul and be aware of its changing power in the fabric of your soul.

Each of us can open up to and approach this evolving power of Gaia in our own way. There is no religion prescribing particular rites. "The New has been here a long time, the Old makes too much noise dying," as German-born author Eckhart Tolle says. This noise resounds throughout the media and drowns out the melody of the awakening Earth, so leave yourself time to engage with it.

The Power of the Serpent
as a Path to Healing

For a number of years now, and in particular as a result of the chaotic upheaval of the pandemic, I have felt an increasingly strong impulse to open portals to Gaia. These are intimately linked to the power of the serpent and form gateways of consciousness and ethereal power to the realms of Gaia. In terms of radiesthesia, I initially used a Lecher antenna (LA) shorting bar length (physical radiesthesia) that also appears in so-called goddess focal points and Earth Mother cult sites (such as in the temples of Ħaġar Qim and Mnajdra on Malta): 4.8 cm (1.9 inches) LA.

Radiesthetic/geomantic research

As Gaia portals (and the power of the serpent that they convey) will play a significant role in transforming the Earth in this current transitional period, and as the power of the serpent can be regarded as virtually the driving force of Earth changes, I thought it appropriate to find a characteristic wavelength that was not also used for themat ically similar phenomena and places.

The wavelengths being emitted at the Gaia portals that were opening up were measured, and the commonly occurring bar lengths were analyzed. Essentially, these are the characteristic bar lengths 2.2 cm (0.9 inches) LA, 3.6 cm (1.4 inches) LA, 4.6 cm (1.8 inches) LA, and the bar length 4.8 cm (1.9 inches) LA already mentioned above. As a rule, 4.6 cm (1.8 inches) LA is encountered with an intensity of 1, the highest intensity, and is thus my preferred length.

The 4.6 cm (1.8 inches) LA power of the serpent can therefore be identified as the driving force of the current changes in the Earth, and signifies a healing stimulus for blocked Earth forces.

A homeopathic approach

During the pandemic, this current era of transformation was characterized by fear and anxiety, including the fear of doing something wrong in an impenetrable maze of regulations and the fear of threats (either from the virus or state intervention). Such anxieties are often linked with a reflex reaction to withdraw from the world and keep to oneself, allowing time to pass and resulting in loneliness.

Interestingly, such fears and emotional reactions are characteristic of two homeopathic remedies, which can therefore be used to soothe and treat them.

Homeopath and author Hans-Jürgen Achtzehn, who has been working as an alternative practitioner since 1984 and is the cofounder of a school of alternative healing, has identified two preparations in particular as being helpful in such fear-filled times: homeopathic remedies derived from the venoms of *Crotalus horridus*, the timber rattlesnake, and *Vipera berus*, the common European viper.

The homeopathic remedy Crotalus Horridus can be used to counteract fear in particular: fear of doing something wrong, fear of being watched or reported to the authorities. It also helps with anger management and powerful stimulation of the nervous system. It can deal with feelings of being under constant threat (such as from the state or a virus), and the insomnia and fatigue that can result.

Vipera Berus counteracts the reflex to withdraw out of fear and helps the sufferer to be proactive instead. It addresses feelings of being at the end of one's tether and the futility of one's own existence in the face of the threatening superiority of Big Brother or an invisible pathogen. It helps to resolve feelings of abandonment by everything and everyone, and delivers a positive sense of connectedness and protection.

Radiesthetic investigation of the preparations

These two snake venoms therefore reflect collective fears and emotional stress very well, and offer their healing power via homeopathy. It is particularly interesting that an analysis of the wavelengths emitted by both homeopathic remedies (apart from their individual frequencies) reveal that they have the following rod lengths in common:

2.2 cm (0.9 inches) LA, 3.6 cm (1.4 inches) LA
4.6 cm (1.8 inches) LA, 4.8 cm (1.9 inches) LA

These wavelengths are the same as those that are characteristic of the power of the serpent at Gaia portals.

The power of the serpent reveals itself as a healing path in the growing conflict between human beings and the Earth, as well as collectively and socially in the current times of great change.

Conversely, wavelengths are also revealed in the vaccine used by many countries in the Western hemisphere, which I had the opportunity to examine radiesthetically. As mentioned earlier, Gaia portals have great significance as ongoing geomantic phenomena in this time of change, and it is interesting to note that the vaccine displayed the two dominant lengths of the Gaia portals (4.6 LA and 4.8 LA) with negative polarization, as if the vaccine were opposing the influence exerted by the portals. The synchronicity of these frequencies occurring is striking: the Lecher value of 4.6 cm (1.8 inches) is found in both the Gaia portals and in dragon paths, and in the homeopathic snake venoms Crotalus Horridus and Vipera Berus, which can both be used to treat fears and anxieties arising during this time. Last but not least, this frequency (let's call it the frequency of serpent/dragon power) in its negative, levorotatory, life-negating polarization, is found in the vaccine most commonly used (at least in Germany) to kill the "dragon virus." As in any dragon battle, however, the dragon—the serpent— will merely shed its skin and be resurrected anew.

A Time of Change:
Opening Dragon Portals

Over the last few chapters, I have referred to the importance of dragons in geomancy in general, and in this transitional period in particular. The dragon powers of the Earth are being released during this time of change, a necessary process given that the powers guarantee the life force within Nature. For too long human beings have inhibited and exploited dragon powers.

So once again my spirit helpers visited me with a request, or rather a demand: to activate 999 dragon portals! Initially, I demurred, as this figure seemed just too great and unachievable. I had activated dragon powers in the Gaia portals, but I had no way of directly opening a portal at that time. I tried to reduce the target amount, suggesting that 99 dragon portals might be sufficient, but my spirit helpers insisted, so I decided to make the ritual opening of a dragon portal part of the initiation week for the current trainee group of Earth guardians.

The date was set for June 10, 2021, at the midday eclipse. During a solar eclipse, the sun and the Black Moon jointly occupy the moon node. The northern (or rising) moon node is also known as the "dragon's head."

The ritual was carried out at an opened Gaia portal, beginning at 12.30 pm. The natural world reacted immediately to the call of the dragons, and the surrounding circle of participants also became aware of the changes right away. Through this ritual opening, I was shown a way to open dragon portals immediately.

When I left the center of the circle and resumed my place once more in the circle of participants, the Earth seemed to be vibrating and pulsating. I began to feel the space-distorting effects of a trance. Around the climax of the eclipse, shortly before 1.00 pm, I was able to make out a kind of golden rain. At the same time, I saw the image of a mighty golden dragon, and everything was radiating a golden light. A blessing seemed to descend upon the Earth.

The skies then began to darken. Since in Bavaria (Germany), coverage of the sun's disc was just 6 percent, it could not have been the moon that was contributing significantly to this effect. All at once, things changed: the "rain" became silver, and a silver dragon arose. After a few minutes, gold and silver both filled the space around me.

It is difficult to determine what part the ritual had played in this experience and what part the eclipse had played, but something had changed around us! Gaia's consciousness had expanded and in the days following the event, daylight seemed different, appearing clear, with greater depth, and almost autumnal.

In this way, all those participating in the shared ritual were now in a position to open dragon portals. As a result, more than fifty portals (that I know of) have since been opened, marking a first step toward the target of 999 portals.

The task of opening 999 dragon portals led me to investigate this rather oddly precise number and to discover more about the mythology surrounding it. The number 999 is a multiple of 9, which is thus raised to a higher power. The number 9 is the last of the natural (counting) single digit numbers. It is the square of 3, which already represents simple perfection; multiplying this number (3) by itself, and the position of the resulting 9 as the last natural number, turns 9 into divine perfection. If we look at the graphical representation of the Arabic numeral 9, which, like all numerals, is drawn around three levels of being—the physical level (lower), the spiritual level (upper), and the ethereal level (middle)—we see that the curve of the "spiral" is rooted in the physical (lower) but bears fruit in the spiritual (upper) level. The number 9 is thus a number that emphasizes the spiritual.

The quality of 9 (divinity or perfection) that is inherent in numbers is constantly revealing itself; each number whose digits add up to 9 is always divisible by 9.

Chinese pagodas ideally have 9 stories and Jesus died in the ninth hour and was deified. The World Tree contains 3 x 3 = 9 worlds, and Odin's self-sacrifice lasted for 9 days and nights. Legend has it that the god Heimdall was born of 9 mothers, and there were 9 choirs of angels in early medieval Christian mythology.

It is also a number of completion and therefore the new beginning of a new level of being. "Nine" has the same etymological roots as "new," and completion and commencement are closely connected in the number.

In Chinese number symbolism, 9 represents the dragon, and in Greek antiquity, the water dragon known as the Hydra was nine-headed (in some versions of the myth). The number is therefore associated with both the heavenly and divine (choirs of angels) and Earth's elemental power (the dragon).

Divinity and elemental power are tripled in the number 999, so it represents even more comprehensively the completion of old cycles while challenging us to abandon the old in order to allow the new to grow out of it. This is why 999 is also known as a master number or angel number, in which dragons and angels meet in perfect harmony.

To this extent, 999 is almost visionary, surpassing the old perfection and allowing the forces of heaven and Earth to merge, bringing the promise of true aid. It is no coincidence that the traditional emergency services number in Great Britain and large parts of the Commonwealth is 999.

There is a message inherent in the call to open 999 dragon portals, calling on humanity to become a bridge between the angelic (astral) world and the earthly elemental plane, and to set aside the dualism of dragon-slaying that we have been living out. The dragon number 9 is enhanced: as with every number divisible by 9, the sum of its digits is also 9 (9+9+9 = 27; 2+7=9). The number 999 frees the mind, just as 666, its graphical inversion, binds it. The dragon portals that have been opened are therefore also a process of spiritual liberation.

The first dragon portal

For the process of opening dragon portals, I was shown a cosmogram that I was to place at opened Gaia portals, and in so doing open a dragon portal.

The cosmogram was engraved onto each of several marble pebbles about the size of a person's fist. Finally, I was allowed to open the first dragon portal with the help of the cosmogram. In terms of which Gaia portal to use for this, it seemed appropriate to choose the first that I had opened; while being the most suitable and harmonious, it was also the most secluded of those that I had opened.

I was very happy to be entering the Gaia portal, as it was clearly perceptible and was pulsating in full presence. The angelic focal point located there was performing a protective role, acting as guardian, and was just as clearly evident, so for the time being I lingered and "bathed" for a while in the wonderful presence of the cosmos and the Earth. It felt good in these unstable times to visit this place of serenity and strength. It showed me once again that politics does not determine everything, and that Gaia goes her own way.

When I saw that the time was right, I placed the cosmogram stone in the shelter of a copse and once again performed the ritual to summon the light of Gaia. I reached deep into the Earth and pulled up a

Fig. 22. The dragon portal cosmogram.

kind of golden ball of light that expanded. At the same time, a part of it focused within the cosmogram stone. It was as if the stone had created a bridge because immediately after this I sensed the dragon power rising. The power manifested itself in the cosmogram stone and then flowed out across the landscape.

The image of a great dragon appeared before my inner eye, stretching and spreading its wings, and then looked directly at me.

All this [the current political/social situation] will not last much longer, I heard its mighty voice say. Humanity must live through what dragon power has had to endure for millennia: subjugation and captivity. Revenge is not the motive, but rather that a seed may be planted in *people's hearts, the seed of a cry for freedom. This need, inherent in every sentient creature, has been almost buried by our everyday lives and our compulsion to consume. As a result, humanity is once more grasping one of the most essential forces of life, and in crying inwardly for life and liberty, we are opening our hearts to it. Perhaps only in this way can we understand what Gaia's life force has had to endure for millennia. The elemental power of life on Earth is the power of the dragon. Set down the stones and free it, free the dragon! With every dragon portal that is opened, more and more of Gaia's elemental power will flow, freeing Nature, plants, animals, the Earth, and ultimately also humanity. The Earth does not need humanity for this process, **but it would very much like humanity to be a part of it!***

As a powerful silence surrounded me, I felt very free at that moment and, through the dragons as messengers of the Earth, felt the power of Gaia flowing into the land. So I stood for a little longer and was drawn to various natural places where I was able to discover the sparkle and vitality of life. It was a profound experience.

A Time of Change: Dreaming of Serpents

We find ourselves in the midst of upheaval in a time of change that will fundamentally transform the Earth, society, and ultimately even our reality. In a process that is frequently difficult to assimilate, even for me, I have found myself turning my attention again and again, sometimes on the verge of sleep, to the current situation and the power of change. I had a short but highly significant dream during the night of November 17, 2020.

I am walking in the countryside with a group of people. We form a circle to talk among ourselves. I notice, in the center of our circle, a shape, which at first I assume to be a stick but which in reality is a serpent. I only just realize this when it rears up in front of me! I look more closely and see that it is not one but two serpents, intertwined as on the caduceus, the staff carried by the god Hermes/Mercury. The two serpents are upright and wrapped around one another as if mating.

Still fascinated by this spectacle, I suddenly notice serpents in other places, on the grass and among the sticks and stones that are lying around on the ground. I can hardly count them all. Are there ten? Twenty? Even more? Where we had just been standing as a group in a circle, I now see snakes everywhere! How did we manage to walk here without stepping on one?

We hardly dare move, but not from fear. Instead, we watch this amazing spectacle with reverence and awe.

Interpreting the dream

The circle
Just as the group in the dream forms a circle, humanity forms a union, a unity that creates a kind of protective circle that brings magic to life. The people form the basis, or rather the framework, quite literally, within which transformation takes place. The protective circle remains intact throughout the entire dream, no one breaks it inadvertently, or out of surprise or fear upon seeing the snakes.

The serpent
As already described, the serpent is an animal of the Earth. It is a symbol of wisdom (Greek *drákōn*, Latin *draco*, similar to "all-seeing, all-knowing animal") Python, the daughter of Gaia, was all-knowing. The serpent represents the power of the consciousness of the Earth. *Vipera* (Latin) derives from *vivipar*, meaning "giving live birth," and so the serpent is a symbol of the life force itself, of Gaia's ability to create life.

Rising up
The serpent, initially in the material guise of an unassuming stick, becomes visible, rises up, and stands vertical. Like the upright form of the Egyptian cobra, this is a symbol of origin and the development of consciousness that arises from it. In a protective circle of people, inanimate matter becomes a development of consciousness, a symbolic connection between heaven and Earth.

Two serpents
One becomes two. Two snakes face each other and entwine their bodies around the caduceus, Hermes' magical staff with the power to transform consciousness. The two entwined serpents have become a global symbol identified with protection and peace, messengers, and peaceful travel into other levels of consciousness. The polarity of yin and yang, the power of the consciousness of the sun and the emotionality of the moon, the mind and the soul, this world and the next, combine to make an uplifting force connecting heaven and Earth.

This dream image is a powerful symbol of the alliance of opposites, and the healing and consciousness-altering power that arises from it.

Many serpents
It is only once the two serpents have raised themselves up that other serpents rise within the circle, as if emerging from the ground, as if the Earth itself was transforming and revealing its serpent form.

Recognition
The circle of people recognizes the natural world, the ground over which they are thoughtlessly trampling, and the scattered sticks that are in fact snakes. People recognize the life-giving power of the consciousness of the Earth that is concealed in Nature. Humbly, they stand by and observe the developing Earth.

This is happening right now. Something is preparing itself, getting ready in the chaos and upheaval of our human society and our personal experience of what has been binding, imprisoning, and exploiting the dragon force for millennia. Something is preparing, indeed something is emerging—the serpent power of the Earth is rising. It is rising in humanity and in Nature. When the tipping point is reached, we will be able to experience this burgeoning power of the Earth directly, and the relationship between humanity and the Earth will change irrevocably!

A Time of Change: Stormy Nights

A hurricane swept across Germany in February 2022 and, although it did not hit Bavaria in southern Germany as hard as elsewhere, the days, and indeed the nights in particular, proved a powerful experience for me. The wind swept through me, even though I remained indoors, seeming to tear out parts of my soul, making me feel agitated and opening me up, and I was very aware of the storm as being more than just a simple movement of air. Once again, powerful changes were taking place, which manifested themselves just a few days later in the conflict in Ukraine.

I found it difficult to concentrate during this time and would frequently wake during the night with no hope of getting back to sleep. I had two particular dreams on these stormy nights.

The first dream: Are you awake?

The first dream occurred immediately before the first wave of the storm hit us. I dreamed that I was asleep. Then I heard a clear voice asking, "Are you awake?" It was as if I had dozed off watching a film and, half asleep, heard the voice. I grunted to indicate somehow that I was awake, which must have translated into real grunting and muttering as it woke me up.

It was about 3.00 am. Try as I might, there was no chance of more sleep, so I worked for about two hours before finally being able to sleep for another hour or so. The day was difficult as a result; the lack of sleep weighed heavily on me and the wind still seemed to be rattling through me.

I decided to take a stroll to try and perk myself up, but the question still echoed around my head. I whispered the words to myself and suddenly, a very bright, wide space opened up around me. Brilliant light streamed through me, and everything around me was flooded with clarity. I somehow sensed the presence of light beings. After a few moments it all faded, but hardly had I whispered "Are you awake?" to myself again when the clear, bright space reopened. It continues to do so to this day whenever I ask myself this same question.

And I do indeed ask myself if I am really awake. Awakening has become a battle cry in the current times, and for that reason I have to answer on a personal level in the negative. No, I'm not awake, but the storm and the question are leading me more and more toward this.

The second dream: The serpent's bite

After the first wave of the storm, I experienced a second disturbed night, which was really very exhausting! I dreamed I was working in a plant nursery. A message was sent round to say that a rattlesnake had been spotted somewhere nearby! Cautiously, we all started to look for it. I spotted it creeping along the floor between some small potted plants and I reached out toward it, entirely free of fear. It coiled in my hands, but it did not look like a rattlesnake. Instead, it resembled a brown adder, with the characteristic diamond pattern on its back. The snake then opened its mouth and bit me between the index finger and thumb of my left hand. At which point, I woke up.

The significance of the serpent as a symbol of the Earth's vitality and power of consciousness has been described at length in this book. In the dream I am completely free of fear. This is interesting in the context because it is specifically the venom of the rattlesnake (*Crotalus horridus*) and the adder (*Vipera berus*) that can be prescribed as homeopathic preparations against the fears of our age (see page 89). The fusion of the two species is apparent in the dream; I go looking for a rattlesnake and find an adder but feel no fear whatsoever (although in reality, I would be absolutely terrified of picking up an adder in that way!). My fears have clearly been allayed. But then the snake bites my left hand.

Our hands are our most important link to the outside world; they allow us to "get to grips" with or "get a handle on" things. We "grasp" reality through the touch of our hands. ("Are you awake?"). I gripped the serpent, the power of the consciousness of the Earth, and perhaps even "grasped" it. I freed myself from fear, and then was bitten on the left hand. The left hand tends to represent the unconscious, emotional side of our nature, the side of the heart, while the right hand is more connected with reasoning.

The bite was right between the index finger and thumb. In t'ai chi tradition, this area is known as the Tiger's Mouth and in acupuncture as Hegu (Converging Valley, LI4). It was as if in biting me here, a point on the Large Intestine meridian, the snake was delivering acupuncture. Stimulation of this point resolves blockages in the body's qi system and the innate qi (the life force) is mobilized and strengthened. Acupuncture releases wind energy (*feng*) in particular and is used to treat the symptoms of a cold. It also alleviates tension and pain, and soothes fears. How much clearer did the dream have to be? What a significant connection! The mobilizing of life force, the dissolution of energetic blockages, the resolution of tension and fear, helping to alleviate cold symptoms . . .

I gratefully accepted the bite, massaged the wound with a circular motion, and asked myself "Are you awake?"

Yes, the storm allayed my fears. It will promote our awakening and connect us more closely with the consciousness of the Earth.

Try this yourself: massage your Hegu point and ask yourself the question "Are you awake?"

Awaken the Dragon Within!

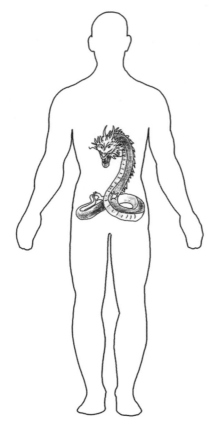

Fig. 23. The dragon within.

The dragon is a symbol of elemental power—within us and within the Earth. It combines the four elements within itself and so becomes the *quinta essentia*, the fifth element. It is the life force per se, the breath of Gaia.

The following energy exercises will help you to become aware of your own dragon power, and to awaken and strengthen it. The geomantic changes that the Earth is currently undergoing show that the Earth's dragon power is becoming increasingly free of the chains that have bound it for millennia. They will prepare you and at the same time support the process.

Exercise

Preparation
- Sit upright or stand.
- The soles of your feet should be in relaxed contact with the floor.

Your physical center and connection to the Earth
- Center yourself. Your center is the space within you in which you are entirely at home with yourself, truly you. Free yourself from any preconceived ideas about where this center has to be.
- Think about where you feel your center is located.
- It could be in your abdomen or your chest.
- Take your time.
- Now imagine a connection from your center to the center of the Earth. It could be a beam of light linking you to the Earth's core.
- In this way, construct a channel between you and the Earth.

Rising soul water
- Now visualize how the soul water of the Earth rises up through this channel.
- Feel how with each breath your body fills more and more with the Earth's soul water.
- Feel how your center absorbs the soul water of the Earth.
- Gaia's soul water is filling and saturating your center like a sponge.
- Allow the soul water of the Earth to continue to rise from below until you (and especially your center) are completely saturated.

The dragon
- Now focus your feelings on your lower abdomen.
- Visualize a dragon curled up and sleeping there.
- Now slowly release the soul water that you have stored in your center.
- Visualize a fine rain falling from your center onto the dragon and running off its scales.

- Visualize the soul water of the Earth bathing the dragon.
- Now feel how the dragon is also being saturated and cleansed by the soul water.
- See how the dragon grows stronger, and slowly, so very slowly, awakens.
- Visualize how it stirs and moves, slowly expanding within you.
- Slowly, very slowly, the dragon within you rises up.
- The dragon touches your solar plexus and eventually also enters your chest.
- Feel the power of the dragon rising up your spine.
- The dragon grows and expands until its presence fills you completely.

The awakened dragon
- Now feel how the cells in your body are receiving the dragon power.
- How does your body feel? How does the dragon's presence alter your perception?
- Feel the energy of the dragon within you.

Repeat this exercise at least once a day.

Picture credits

Fig. 1, 3, 4: Fotolia
2: zebra0209/shutterstock
4 (Hermes), 5, 7, 9, 12, 13a/1: historic, public domain
6: Shanshan0312/shutterstock
8, 13a/2, 13b, 14, 15, 16, 18, 20, 21, 22: Stefan Broennle
10a: Tangopaso/Wikipedia, public domain
10b: Sibylle Krähenbühl
11, 23: Arson Krähenbühl
17: Thinkstock
19: Leif Brönnle

Vignettes:
Pages 9, 25: Furqan248/shutterstock.com
26, 46: ArtoPhotoDesigno Studio/shutterstock.com
47, 55 (dragon of the national flag of Wales): public domain
56, 79: Insima/dreamstime.com
80, 105, 106, 108: ArtCreationsDesignPhoto/shutterstock.com

About the Author

Stefan Broennle is a geomantic consultant and engineer. He studied landscape ecology at the Technical University of Munich and has been providing consultancy and design services for interior and exterior spaces since 1993.

His focus is not simply on incorporating physical radiesthesia but also, more importantly, on the concrete spiritual relationship between person and place, which is supported through ritual practices and shaped and structured by the energetic power of rocks (lithoenergy), water (hydroenergy), and plants (phytoenergy).

Since 1994 he has been a course leader and lecturer, first for HAGIA CHORA and now for INANA school of geomancy, both of which he co-founded. He has held a lectureship at Weihenstephan-Triesdorf University since 2011.

He has also trained in Qi Gong, Taijiquan, radiesthesia, technical remote viewing (TRV), and focusing. He lives in Germany and is passionate about bringing together the physical and spiritual aspects of geomancy.

This oracle set offers a hands-on way to connect with the spiritual wisdom of dragons. Each of the 43 cards features beautiful artwork to allow you to activate dragon energies and use them on an intuitive level. The guidebook details the message of each card and offers meditative journeys into the world of dragons.

Christine Arana Fader
Dragon Wisdom
43-Card Oracle Deck and Book
Includes 112-page book and 43 full-color cards
ISBN 978-1-64411-108-6

This powerful book with its beautiful illustrations allows you to enter the mystical world of dragons. Once you are ready, it will help you get to know your own dragon, your close personal companion, and to share its invincibility, wisdom, and magic.

Christine Arana Fader
The Little Book of Dragons
Finding your spirit guide
Paperback, full-color throughout, 120 pages
ISBN 978-1-84409-670-1

Dragons, the oldest creatures in our universe, have accompanied gods, goddesses, planets, angels, elves, and ascended masters through the ages. In this 43-card full-color deck and guidebook set, Christine Arana Fader introduces us to the dragon riders and the profound spiritual love and support they have to offer.

Christine Arana Fader
The Dragon Riders Oracle
43-Card Deck and Book
Includes 112-page book and 43 full-color cards
ISBN 979-8-88850-073-6

The 12 nights following the winter solstice—Yuletide—offer the ideal opportunity for inner focusing, for seeing signs, and for planting seeds for the future. This book shares reflective themes and exercises for each night (and the day to follow) and guided meditations to deepen the experience.

Anne Stallkamp, Werner Hartung
Inner Practices for the Twelve Nights of Yuletide
Paperback, 144 pages
ISBN 978-1-64411-324-0

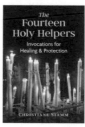

For further information and to request a book catalogue contact:
Inner Traditions, One Park Street, Rochester, Vermont 05767

Earthdancer Books is an Inner Traditions imprint.
Phone: +1-800-246-8648, customerservice@innertraditions.com
www.earthdancerbooks.com • www.innertraditions.com

EARTHDANCER

AN INNER TRADITIONS IMPRINT